5-7-73

Historians and
the open society

Historians and the open society

A R Bridbury

Department of Economic History,
London School of Economics

Routledge & Kegan Paul
London and Boston

First published 1972
by Routledge & Kegan Paul Ltd
Broadway House, 68–74 Carter Lane,
London EC4V 5EL and
9 Park Street,
Boston, Mass. 02108, U.S.A.
Printed in Great Britain by
Clarke, Doble & Brendon Ltd
Plymouth

ISBN 0 7100 7337 2

Contents

1766287

Preface

The author of *Ecce Homo* was driven by the reaction of some of his critics to the tone of confident dogmatism that they professed to find in his writing to submit a modest disclaimer in the fifth edition which so exactly expresses my own feelings that I am constrained to quote it here.

> Dogmatism is no doubt used by superiors to inferiors, but it is also used in conversation between people who feel themselves perfectly equal. Expressions of modest deference, confessions of fallibility and imperfect knowledge are wearisome between equals. The writer addresses throughout free inquirers like himself, and uses the tone which he would like others to adopt towards him. His book is not a book of authority, but of inquiry and suggestion; it is intended not to close discussion, but to open it.

Throughout the following pages the phrase 'the historian' is used as a concession to brevity, and not by any means as a comprehensive indictment of everyone who writes history. And the book itself is addressed to those reasonable men and women with a taste for history who, in politics, are weary of the mendacious claims of the protagonists of left and right, who value the libertarian ideals that both sides claim exclusively for themselves, and who are fearful for the future of liberty.

Introduction

Historians who live in the world's liberal democracies have every inducement to lead double lives. Victorian pillars of society proclaimed the sanctity of hearth and home, idealized the purity of their wives and daughters, and slept with pretty housemaids on the sly. Sexual morals, for all their tumultuous complexity, have now lost that particular kind of tortuosity. Historians are tempted professionally. They proclaim the sanctity of the democratic process, idealize liberty, and yet, when they turn to their professional work, promptly disown their political beliefs and forswear the values upon which these beliefs depend.

They subscribe wholeheartedly to the belief that the political system is, or should be, a free partnership of men and women who nevertheless differ from one another in every conceivable way, and to the belief that such differences should on no account be allowed to compromise the equal status of all members of the partnership before the law, their equal rights in politics, and their equal access to opportunities for advancement in public life, business, and the professions. To crown all, they subscribe to the further belief that nothing but the constraints imposed by neighbourliness and the calls of social obligation should prevent anyone from living life as he wishes to do and making whatever he pleases of it.

Surely no compound of liberalism and egalitarianism could be conceived of which was more unstable or potentially more explosive than this one. It calls for the harnessing of the fraternal and conciliatory impulses and the liberation of the individualistic and idiosyncratic ones. It requires self-discipline and social discipline, and yet it cannot dispense with competition without sacrificing a vital medium of self-expression and one of the chief safeguards of the liberty of the subject. Willing the end, liberal democrats are presumably content to will the means. And historians who subscribe to the theory of liberal democracy are consequently committed to a profound faith in a variety of humane and egalitarian values and to the profound conviction that what a man does or says or thinks or feels is, at bottom, very much his own business and no-one else's.

When they turn to the past, however, historians are irresistibly tempted to betray their complex and somewhat whimsical political and social beliefs. When they turn to the past, it is not with the austerely dispassionate eye that sees but does not judge; nor is it with the compassionate heart that judges by the standards of the time and the temptations of the moment : all too frequently it is with the mawkish rapture of the sycophant for whom scarcely anything is so bad that success cannot redeem it.

It is not difficult to understand why they are so irresistibly tempted. The past leaves few traces. Thoughts, feelings, and actions, are fugitive things that rarely make a mark indelible enough to be transmitted to posterity. And when they do, how badly they travel! The historian is heir to no rich heritage. He is a beachcomber, more than content when he is fortunate enough to be a 'snapper-up of unconsidered trifles'. In the welter of mischances, utterly random contingencies, and rare strokes of good fortune, which determine the provisioning of his stock of materials, certain events, and certain personages, stand out. The historian clings gratefully to these and makes them central to his theme. On the whole the people with whom he deals have done well for themselves. They belong to the dominant classes and control the dominant institutions. The historian steeps himself in their affairs; relishes their triumphs; extenuates their mistakes; deplores their misfortunes; and presently finds himself taking them at their own valuation. In this way the concept of success insinuates itself into the historian's mind, where it thrives to such effect that eventually success becomes the touchstone of his scale of values. From the point where the historian recognizes greatness and rejoices to see it succeed, the descent is steep and rapid to the point where he sees success and calls it greatness, and to the further point where he discovers that overwhelming power is its own justification, whether in men or in institutions, whether in nations or in businesses.

Accordingly he welcomes movements which strengthen powers that are already considerable. He takes the keenest pleasure in the growth of nationalism, which turns a rabble of heterogeneous forces into an army of organized purposes, and deprecates irredentism, except as a hopeless gesture, for its disruptive effect upon the forward march of history. Centralization, since it makes government stronger, has no terrors for him. Nor can he speak too highly of those masterful men who modernize the machinery of government so as to make centralization more effective. His loyalties, indeed, are wholeheartedly committed to those who exercise the controlling powers in the community. When he turns to the details of politics his concern is chiefly with the public quarrels of the affluent classes. When he contemplates the constitution he reflects mainly upon the rules that the affluent classes evolved so as to regulate the way in which these public quarrels were to be conducted. When he writes social history it turns out to be, more than anything else, an account of how the affluent classes lived when they were not quarrelling in public. When he writes economic history he does so in the belief that his duty is done when he has shown how profitably the resources of the economy were exploited for their own ends by those who were quick, clever, lucky, or unscrupulous enough, to seize their chance of fame and fortune when it came. And when he looks beyond the frontiers of the individual community to the wider world of interacting communities that constitutes the framework of his scheme of things, he extols the authority of the dominant power and the ascendancy of the dominant economy with as much enthusiasm as ever and for the same reasons as before.

His preoccupation with success measured in these terms means that the historian scarcely notices the people who have occupied the villages and thronged the towns since time began. He is not concerned to investigate the realities of politics as they bore down on them. He does not ask what the law of the land actually meant in the regions and the localities. His interest in economic affairs generally lapses at the point where questions are raised as to the terms upon which the rich and powerful were pleased to grant to the rest of the community its access to the resources of the economic system, and hence its access to the means with which to increase the well-being of all.

And yet without pursuing the social, economic, and political consequences of the achievements of those whom he admires so ardently, how can the historian possibly justify the lavish tribute he pays them? Throughout history those who have managed to help themselves liberally to the world's goods and the world's prizes have rarely bothered themselves with the further consequences of policies and activities which have rewarded them so well. The historian is notably reluctant to follow his investigations through, and judge his heroes, if he must judge them at all, not so much by what they did for themselves as by the consequences of what they did for everyone else. And his reluctance to do so is surely a measure of his enslavement to standards of value which are common enough amongst the general run of the famous and the successful but which he himself finds repugnant in politics and which his professional code of impartiality in these matters does not require him to uphold.

His reluctance to probe the achievements of the men and movements to which he has devoted himself, owes nothing to the dearth of materials with which to handle such investigations. Indeed if the materials were deficient then judgment could no more go by default in their favour than it could go against them. And in fact the materials often survive abundantly enough. Sometimes they survive embedded in extraneous matter which promises only a low yield in return for much quarrying. But this is by no means always so. His natural disposition to work accessible seams first cannot be the historian's excuse for neglecting to probe more deeply than he does : for the materials with which he tells his success stories often reveal, if only by implication, much of what must be known and weighed before these stories can be told as he tells them.

In short the historian's unshakable and inflexible preoccupation is with interests; and these he measures along a scale which gives primacy to those which have not only achieved outstanding success in their own day, but can also be represented as having made an outstanding contribution to the task of preparing society for its culminating moment, which is always the present. This is the Whig interpretation of history with a vengeance. Hunted out of certain prominent lodgments by Professor Butterfield, it has found a natural refuge in others, amongst which, lodgments in social and economic history are now conspicuous. The historian who begins by distorting the past for the sake of the successful men and women who dominate his vision of it thus ends up by falsifying the process of change in order to give them a leading part in it.

And what a shrine he raises to the sanctified butchers and racketeers, the immortal masters of terror and brutality, perjury and intrigue, the common delinquents vindicated by uncommon achievements, who crowd his pages! Uninhibited rapacity honoured in terms of the antiquated bombast of imperialism; violent repression of minorities excused in the name of national unification; comprehensive despotism in matters of conduct and over the expression of opinions concerning problems upon which no two authorities have ever succeeded in giving unconflicting commentaries, justified by the magnificence of the outward splendours of medieval theocracy; gigantic conspiracies against the public interest disguised as colonial policy and invested with the romance of the rise of maritime enterprise; the costs of war depreciated or altogether concealed, its tangible benefits extolled as intemperately as earlier generations had extolled its glamour; nice problems of the effects of industrialization upon society and upon living standards prudently narrowed so as to exclude all reference to the slavery upon which so much depended; mercantilism, as resurrected by industrialized nations, glorified for its effect upon the output of products which did more to terrorize rivals and neighbours than to increase the wealth or comfort of the populace; empire-building, no longer fashionable in politics, now eulogized in business; and heroes everywhere, provided that their lives have been conducted with suitably garish ostentation and their careers have been crowned with success. For this purpose the canon can be extended in one direction to embrace the loathsomely repulsive neurotic who backs into the limelight with fastings and scourgings of the flesh, and in the other to include the sublimely illustrious statesman who makes his supreme sacrifice, as Thomas à Becket did, with the utmost publicity and in circumstances of flamboyant melodrama.

If the test of a society is the quality of its heroes, who can say much for ours? And yet when have prospects been fairer? The wealth generated by industrialism and augmented by international trade has driven from western Europe the want and pain and degradation that crushed untold generations in the past. Traditional problems recede as poverty comes to mean stinted comforts instead of destitution; physical health is taken for granted; and the enforced idleness that once corrupted or broke those who could not find work, loses its separate identity in the general problem of finding ways to fill the extended leisure made possible for all by the new abundance. Fresh problems will, no doubt, soon clamour for attention. Wealth never yet reconciled any man to his lot. If history is 'the register of the crimes, follies, and misfortunes of mankind', then it is, as it is now written, very much the register of the crimes and follies committed by those well supplied with the comforts and consolations of life, and accorded, in full measure, the deference paid to great possessions. And it would be ingenuous to a degree to suppose that the sons and daughters of the old poor, now that they are the new rich, will not respond to their opportunities as the rich always have done, and will not commit crimes and follies comparable with anything done by their betters in days gone by. Moreover, annihilating war broods over the industrially advanced countries as pestilence and famine once did. But the economic and social destinies of western Europe are in the hands of the peoples of western Europe as they never were before. If their future is not as brilliant as their past was forbidding, then the peoples of western Europe will have no-one to blame but themselves.

What should they make of their opportunities? If they allow race or creed to be a barrier between them, or between themselves and others; if they breed excessively; if they follow their modish Old Testament prophets into the theological bondage of the politics of right or left; if they pander to the vested interests that would sacrifice their freedom upon the altar of national power; if they throw out-door relief to poorer neighbours instead of offering them markets for their goods; then the future will hold few surprises for them : it will be very much like the past.

But there is an alternative. Whilst the super-powers are preparing an unimaginable holocaust for mankind, there is time, perhaps, for a brief interlude of civilization. Civilization is not simply a question of law and order, though civilization would be impossible without them. Nor is it another name for a state of affairs in which the fine arts are able to flourish. The suggestion that it is, carries with it the unpleasant innuendo that ordinary men and women are merely dung in which roses bloom; and in countries where the equal status of all is one of the fundamental tenets of political faith, civilization is surely incompatible with any form of social organization which could, if necessary, relegate ordinary people to a helot's role. Would it not be true, indeed, to say that, in such countries, civilization is very much a question of the social virtues? In the liberal communities of western Europe, a region where so many of the world's masterpieces of creative thought and feeling have been wrought, strenuous thought is at last being given to the task of creating a social environment which can turn the brotherhood of man into a political reality without stifling the personal dignity and independence of the individual. If the people of western Europe can make a practical reality of their political ideals, they will have achieved a masterpiece of thought and behaviour as remarkable as anything achieved by their forbears in the fine arts. If they succeed, would it be wrong to describe the result as civilization?

Formidable difficulties lie ahead in communities in which, for all their sophistication, tribal warfare simmers an inch below the surface, and the pressure to conform is finding, in business and education, fresh means with which to maintain its customary intensity. Moreover, if poverty is one kind of bondage, wealth is another. Poverty cannot; wealth dares not. Timidity is the curse of possessions, and possessions are the enemy of political reform. Those with possessions preach empiricism as a way of resisting change. Consequently as wealth accumulates, change becomes harder than ever to bring about without violent disruption. Meanwhile the barriers raised or hallowed by extremists at either end of the political spectrum are built higher than ever against the kind of reform that would rid the community of the conspiracies against the public interest increasingly fomented by business and the professions, by the trades unions and by government itself, which is driven as much by the gathering momentum of its own power as by the propulsion imparted to it by those who have succeeded in using it to promote their own ends. The life of freedom and civilization that is the promise of liberal democracy is not easy to achieve even when poverty, sickness, and the anxieties they cause, are no longer impediments to it.

There is little enough that the historian can do to help. History may 'hold children from play and old men from the chimney corner', but it has no useful social function to perform in the sense that it can shed light where clues as to the causes of things are to be found. It has not earned, and cannot earn, the authority that it commands in certain quarters as a fund of sociological insights. Nor can its prophetic quality serve the purposes that sociology aspires to achieve. 'The first lesson of history', said the late G. M. Young,[1] 'and it may well be the last, is that you never know what is coming next.' Nevertheless social consequences are bound to flow from any attempt to pursue the problems, revive the passions, and re-create the antagonisms, of past ages. And history has often enough inspired men and nations to surrender themselves to fatal ambitions, or preyed upon them, and daunted them from making any attempt to do what they might easily have accomplished. No doubt people take from history very largely what they want to find in history. But to the extent that history can exert a formative influence, its influence in the liberal communities, at this momentous juncture of human history, ought not to give comfort to those who, intentionally or not, are strengthening the forces that make it impossible for liberal democracy to grow to full stature, and hard for it to survive.

[1] *Victorian Essays*, ed W. D. Handcock, Oxford University Press, 1962, p. 10.

1 War, bureaucracy, and constitutional development: some neglected costs

Anniversaries are a bore because a year gives one so brief a respite from their recurrence. Prolonging the interval buys respite at the cost of heightening the tension. Centenaries are thus made intolerable by the sense of occasion that incites otherwise perfectly rational men and women to fatuous outbursts of sentimentality and idolatry. The ninth centenary of the Norman Conquest, recently celebrated, ran true to form. The sentimentalists and idolators performed their appointed rituals, capering foolishly round the monument they had raised to 'the Conqueror'; seeing the England of Shakespeare, and Chatham, and the Railway Age, in the squalid brutalities of a gang of Norman marauders; despising the Saxons because their voice was silenced and their culture choked; and eagerly attributing genius to the lucky throw of an adventurer who but for the coincidence of a northern invasion with his own, which distracted Harold and exhausted his men at the crucial moment, might very well have found himself stranded on a lee shore in a hostile land with overwhelming forces gathering to destroy him. 'The ultimate fact of victory', as Liddell Hart said about Blenheim, 'sufficed to make the world overlook what a gamble the battle had been.'[1]

Luck, it is said, favours those who are prepared. But luck is not a just and terrible god, and no sane man reflecting upon the course of history can surely fail to be revolted by the egregious complacency that assumes that it is. If luck gave Napoleon a wife who could get him his chance of glory by making herself agreeable to the Directory, it also gave Gladstone Parnell as the ally of the great enterprise of his later years. If it gave Elizabeth Tudor

[1] B. H. Liddell Hart, *Strategy: The Indirect Approach*, Faber, 1967, p. 100.

B

an iron constitution, it also snuffed out Keats before he was twenty-six years old. It deprived England of the effective political services of one of the most gifted men ever to enter her public life by withholding crucial qualities from the richly-endowed personality of Charles James Fox; and granted Disraeli what it had denied Fox without granting him also the distinction of mind and purpose that raised Fox as high above Disraeli in moral concern as Disraeli stood above Fox in profound and enduring political influence. It did incalculable and probably irreparable harm to France by giving Louis VII a wife who succumbed to the magnetism of Henry of Anjou, transferred herself and her Duchy of Aquitaine to the lover who subsequently became King of England, and thus created the ganglion in the flesh of France that festered for centuries, poisoning social and political relationships in more ways than historians have yet explored.

Indeed the memory and imagination of the race are so crowded with dramatic illustrations of 'the play of the contingent and the unforeseen' that multiplying examples should serve no purpose beyond that of labouring the obvious. But the obvious has no influence over the kind of obsession that sees bold initiative in every blind risk; foresight and calculation where there was only desperate improvisation against time; knowledge and intelligence where in fact ignorant and credulous men had been rescued from the consequences of their own shortcomings by resourceful but anonymous and devoted subordinates; the granite virtues where there was nothing but stolid perversity of temperament; and subtlety and freedom from cant where there was treachery, fraudulence, and lies. In short the working historian who prides himself upon his contempt for philosophy and cherishes the belief that he is, above all, an empiricist, is, in fact, a martyr to the romantic yearnings that betray him into concocting heroes out of the prosaic ingredients of his craft.

To the dispassionate observer it is tolerably clear that late Saxon society was a culturally sophisticated and constitutionally mature society with as much of a civilian caste to it as those unquiet times would permit. The Normans did not bring England into Europe. For what it was worth, England was European already. The Normans could teach the Anglo-Saxons nothing about finance and administration. The nation that produced the Domesday Book within a generation of the Conquest had nothing to learn from the Duke's men in these matters. What the Normans did, surely, was to militarize and degrade the country. The claim that they revived and restored a decadent and enfeebled society rests, not upon evidence, but upon the belief that failing the ordeal of battle is as decisive as a test of social debility as it once was as a proof of legal guilt.

Historians writing in the meridian of empire could applaud the colonizers with fewer qualms than are felt today : in the sunset hour it should be easier to see the point of view of the colonials. But what is significant about modern treatment of the Conquest, and of its hero, the Conqueror, is not its quest for a change of perspective : it is the inflexible determination to see success as the sanctifying agency in history.

Success, however, needs closer definition. Specialization, which has resolved so many activities into their constituent parts, has at once emancipated and imprisoned the historian by dissolving the unity of history into a congeries of unrelated disciplines. Each of these disciplines has its own criterion of success.

To the military historian success means victory. The great strategist is not the man whose plans look best; he is the man whose plans work. And the campaigns that matter are not the ones that start well, or go according to plan; they are the campaigns that bring wars to a successful conclusion. Defeat can be glorious just as victory can be despicable. But military history pauses briefly, if at all, over the shattered ranks of the defeated, however noble their cause or selfless their sacrifice. Its business is with those who win, however odious they or their cause may be. Victory may not yield the results that war was embarked upon to achieve. Again the military historian is unmoved. His test of professional skill is simple and compelling. And indeed it would be difficult to imagine a satisfactory test of military skill which did not concede to the man who wins without having the odds loaded in his favour, some claim to excellence which must be denied to his defeated adversary. But the military historian does not discriminate between the great victory and the great commander. For his purposes the greater the victory, the greater the commander. Cost does not concern him. Only the commander who fails in the end, despite brilliant successes, or who wins only because attrition works for him rather than against him, has to answer for the casualty list and take the blame for the financial strains, the material losses and the social costs that his campaigns have incurred.

This is surely an extraordinary abdication of judgment by the military historian who is, apparently, so much the victim of his enthusiasms as to forget that in war, as in everything else, success has its price, and that unless he takes into account the price at which success was bought he cannot possibly tell whether success was worth the price that had to be paid for it.

The grim story is now well-known of how Liddell Hart, a subaltern veteran of the carnage of the war of 1914–18, set to work to explain to his fellow-countrymen the strategy of indirect approach upon which quick, cheap, and decisive victory has always depended, only to find that he had succeeded in explaining it to his country's enemies, with sensational results which were very nearly fatal to his country's cause. If he had little enough influence upon the generals and the cabinet ministers for whom he wrote, and sometimes worked, he seems to have had even less influence upon the historians, whose accounts of the great commanders display no recognition of the truth, to which his books bore witness, that a war won at devastating cost is not a war won at all. The world's appetite for famous victories and for un-tarnished heroes, however, imposes upon even the most critical intellects, and nothing demonstrates this more vividly than the fact that even Liddell Hart never quite emancipated himself from an infatuation with the career of the successful commander which could betray him, occasionally, into defending the wild gamble that came off and the costly victory that was not worth the winning.

To the administrative historian the successful administrator is the man who gets things done, the successful administration, the administration in which the office is coherently organized, the chain of command is clear and intelligible, and the work dis-patched without fuss or delay. Since office work is something that we believe we do better than it has ever been done before, the administrative historian's standards are unashamedly those of today, and he praises the modernizer, the man who sets up in rudimentary form an organization which looks recognizably like the ones we have now. He never asks whether efficient dis-patch of business was the central purpose of the administration he studies, or the true need of the political system of which it was a minor element. He relishes Bright's devastating sarcasm about the mid-Victorian Foreign Office, that it was nothing but a 'gigantic system of outdoor relief for the aristocratic classes'; but he does not take Bright's point : for administrative history is never written so as to stress the predominant part so often played by patronage in the evolution and, still more, in the utilization of those improved techniques of office management that preoccupy the historian. Nor is he disquieted by the improvements that modernization achieved. The administrative reformers of the seventeenth century looked abroad to Louis XIV and Colbert with envy, and preferred Hobbes to Locke. It is not surprising that they should have done so. Administrative reform makes government more effective. But the historian who readily endorses such reform and therefore welcomes the additional power it confers upon government makes larger assumptions about the benefits dispensed by government than are warranted either by his duties as an historian or by his own convictions about politics.

In this respect his affinity is with the constitutional historian who adds an obsession with forms and precedents to the predilection for coherence and efficiency, uniformity and central control that he shares with the administrative historian. The constitutional historian's preoccupation is with structure rather than process : with the anatomy of power rather than with its pathology. His dominant themes are king and parliament; his chief concern to depict the sovereignty of the king in the days when kings ruled as well as reigned, and to trace the measured growth of parliament and chronicle the irresistible expansion and burgeoning of its power once the king had been eclipsed.

When government depended upon the king, the king had to be strong. And to be strong he had to be an able general or clever enough to avoid entanglements which might reveal the deficiencies of his generalship. He also had to be financially independent. And the constitutional historian's admiration and esteem for the strong king who lived of his own is almost boundless. The king who lived of his own was not shackled by paymasters. He was not hampered by the need to redress grievance. If he summoned parliament, his doing so was an act of grace and a sign of strength, not the last resort of a bankrupt. And should parliament prove to be recalcitrant the strong king knew how to charm, cajole, or intimidate it into doing his bidding, and when to send it about its business and rule without its help. He might be a bloody tyrant outraging even indulgent contemporary standards of public morality. His constitutional innovations might be nothing but a string of squalid extemporizations which impressed neither his enemies nor even those who worked with him and benefited from his patronage. But if he were strong, and if his innovations could be woven into a coherent pattern, then his honoured place in constitutional history was assured.

Unfortunately for himself, the constitutional historian cannot make the theme of the masterful king last the whole story through. No sooner has he established the Tudor king as the culminating perfection of the type, than he is forced to abandon king for parliament and to tell another story, the story of the growth of parliamentary government. In the Middle Ages only feeble and inadequate kings depended upon parliament; and parliamentary power, great at moments, is depicted in such a way as to make it a sad commentary upon their mediocrity and incompetence. By the seventeenth century things are quite different. The old tricks that enabled earlier kings to manage the country have become shabby and disreputable, at least to the historian who knows that they will fail. Consequently the successful king no longer hectors or beguiles : he signs the Bill of Rights and submits himself, more or less meekly, to a humbler and more circumscribed role.

In the event his submission proves to be formal rather than substantial. One-party government and a firm hand with parliament give him a longer lease than he could have bargained for on the morrow of submission. But parliament's day was dawning; and the constitutional historian presently feels free to extol the virtues of parliament, to venerate its complex ancestry and rich traditions, and to applaud its brilliant promise.

This passion for backing the winner at all costs betrays the constitutional historian into manipulating his evidence in a variety of ways of which three are outstanding.

The constitutional historian has the lawyer's faith in precedents. They enshrine and guarantee the victories of constitutional history. Precedents, however, are legion. Not all of them are admirable. Some indeed are abhorrent. But these, providentially, lack the stamina of the precedents that serve the purposes of constitutional development. Either they fade away or they can be explained away. They are not true precedents. True precedents, moreover, are not merely robust. They have other qualities. In particular they have the sovereign merit of being exempt from malicious distortion or honest misrepresentation. None ever seems to have its plain intention nullified by skilful advocacy, perfunctory compliance, or by a tacit but universal conspiracy to ignore its tenor and meaning. In this respect constitutional precedents are, apparently, exempt from the fate that has overtaken the Ten Commandments, the Sermon on the Mount, the Constitution of the U.S.A., and all the other monuments to mankind's attempts to root its aspirations in the soil. They shine out like stars, austere and immutable witnesses to the inexorable progression of constitutional affairs from one stage of enlightenment to the next.

But if he is ingenuous as to the integrity of his precedents, the constitutional historian is positively abject in his idolatry of institutions. He takes institutions at face value, content, apparently, to ignore the intense and unremitting social pressures that make the working reality of institutions vastly different from their appearance. His admiration for the jury system, for example, is unqualified. In this he is not alone. Nor is he alone in never having submitted the workings of the jury system to critical scrutiny. When a recent government restored a medieval precedent, by authorizing majority verdicts, it provoked a public controversy which revealed more plainly, perhaps, than anything else could have done, that we have no systematic knowledge whatsoever of the way in which the jury system works, and consequently of its sanity, objectivity, and efficacy as an instrument of justice. Sheer survival has hallowed the jury system and canonized its mysteries. We serve it with incense instead of eyeing it dispassionately as social reformers. The constitutional historian carries this attitude of credulous adulation back into the past, to days when the regions of England were ruled by Olympian magnates and dominated by their satellite local bosses; when the jury system was, therefore, very probably the most perfect instrument of legalized intimidation and fraud then known to man. And he sustains his faith in trial by jury by studiously ignoring its social context and concentrating doggedly upon its formalities.

But these deficiencies are trifling incidental improprieties compared with the chief fault of constitutional history, which is its fundamental irrelevance to the history of the public rights and obligations of the overwhelming majority of the people of England. We smile patronizingly at the Liberian constitution which manages to look something like the American one without in fact conceding a shred of representation to nine-tenths of the population, which it keeps poor, and ignorant, and docile, for the sake of the tiny oligarchy that battens on it. Yet if we banish national pride from our minds can we honestly claim that the constitution of England was so very different until recent times? What were the epic contests of king and barons and king and parliament but the family quarrels of the ruling classes? And what were the ruling classes but the tiny oligarchy that controlled England in the days of Gregory King and Patrick Colquhoun as it had done when Domesday Book was being compiled and Magna Carta signed?

In this respect England was not exceptional. Over the greater part of Europe politics and the constitution were exclusively the preserve of men of substance. The fruits of constitutional development, like the triumphs of politics, were the monopoly of those with money and education and influence. The mass of the inhabitants of the countries of Europe could make themselves felt when occasion offered, but knew nothing of the liberty of the subject, except, perhaps, as an idle phrase, or of representative government, except as yet another perquisite of the enfranchised few.

It would be wrong to depict English society, at any period, as being rigidly stratified into rich and poor, master and servant, aristocrat and retainer. Its interpenetrations were numerous and intricate. Where the casual eye saw nothing but villages of undifferentiated peasants, a more discerning one might see baffling social complexities: copyholders with very much more than a competence; freeholders close to subsistence; men of no great substance or quality with copyhold, and leasehold, as well as freehold land, to their credit; and not a few combining the occupations of farmer, casual labourer, and self-employed artisan, and in one or other of these capacities employing labour perhaps, and knowing the problems of business, therefore, from both sides. In the towns where opportunities were greater, variations of status, occupation, and wealth, could be even more complex than they were in the villages. Moreover the social system itself was in constant movement. Class never hardened into caste. At one extreme riches bought gentility; at the other, poverty hurried its victims to social annihilation and, possibly, to utter ruin. And the process of absorption into higher classes, or rejection and decline into lower ones, never ceased.

But movements such as these were very much on the fringe of things. In every age until the Victorian, except, perhaps, for golden interludes in later medieval times, and in the century between the Restoration and the accession of George III, periodic starvation and chronic illness were the common lot. And until their menace receded permanently, impenetrable social barriers inevitably segregated the labouring poor, who made up the bulk of the population, from the middle and upper classes. Social ostracism may be racial today; until very recently it was a matter of class. Profound and irreconcilable differences of wealth and education, customs and habits, divided the classes as they now divide the races. How deep they ran it is exceedingly difficult for anyone living in twentieth-century England to appreciate. The peasant's helpless ignorance, his social and physical degradation, wretchedness, and squalor, made him as unfit for the society of landlord and employer as his problems and needs kept him remote from their range of compassionate sympathy, and, hence, beyond the limits of their willingness to help. Industrialization did not create the Two Nations; it simply altered their polarity. In nineteenth-century England, Gladstone alone, amongst statesmen of the first rank, understood the problems these disparities created. And the feeling persisted even amongst humane men that the poor were an irrevocably degraded rabble. De Tocqueville looking at Manchester in 1835 saw a town where 'civilization works its miracles and civilized man is turned almost into a savage.'[2] Leonard Woolf, recalling his childhood in late Victorian London,[3] echoed de Tocqueville by describing London as a place where, 'under the prim and pious pattern of bourgeois life, just beneath the surface of society, lay a vast reservoir of uncivilized squalor and brutality which no longer exists. No one but an old Londoner . . . can have any idea of the extent of the change.'

The white South African or Southern-States American who denies his black fellow-countrymen access to the better-paid jobs, bars them from careers in politics, and then argues that the black races must be inferior because they do only menial work, and

[2] De Tocqueville, *Journeys to England and Ireland*, ed J. P. Mayer, Faber, 1958, pp. 103–8.
[3] Leonard Woolf, *Sowing*, Hogarth Press, 1961, p. 58.

behave irresponsibly unless watched, is the true descendant of those who used their wealth and political influence to keep the labouring poor in bondage and then argued that people who could not break their bonds were not fit to exercise public responsibilities.

The social realities that the rich and powerful so energetically confirmed, sank deep into political thought. When medieval Englishmen spoke of the community of the realm they did not mean all the adult male inhabitants of the kingdom. In the towns they meant the ruling oligarchies. In the countryside they meant the magnates and the county families. Indeed the conviction that only men of unquestionably independent means could be trusted with political power runs right through the orthodox traditions of later political thought. It took many generations before an alternative theory was evolved, and longer still before alternative practices prevailed. Even the most radical of English political thinkers, the Levellers, in the most radical of English centuries, the seventeenth century, proposed a franchise which would have given the suffrage to no more than twice the proportion of adult males that actually had it in 1688. And their reasons for so timid a departure from orthodoxy show that they differed from orthodox views not in theory, but merely over a matter of fact. They assumed, as the orthodox thinkers did not, that the average tenant-farmer, whether copyholder or leaseholder, was independent of the will of other men in a way in which the wage-earner and the pauper were not. Their assumption was surely wrong, and showed the sort of ignorance of contemporary life that is usually imputed to reactionary rather than to progressive thinkers. The average tenant-farmer, oppressed by debt to the point of being a mere hireling of the local usurer, his tenure at the mercy of a landlord's whim whatever the protection that the law might seem to afford, his obligations often mounting against him, was not presumably less amenable to undue influence than the next man. And Cromwell and Ireton were surely right to contest the Levellers' proposal, on the ground that if property were to be the guarantee of political integrity, then the ordinary tenant-farmer was not, in the sense that mattered, a man of property.[4]

[4] C. B. Macpherson, *The Political Theory of Possessive Individualism,* Oxford University Press, 1962, *passim*; J. H. Plumb, *The Growth of Political Stability in England, 1675–1725,* Macmillan, 1967, p. 29.

In these circumstances representative government and the rule of law meant nothing to the mass of the population. How could the landed gentry represent the farm labourer and the wage-earning artisan? And indeed it never occurred to them to do so. Burke no more had the common people in mind when he defended the idea of representation before the electors of Bristol in 1774 than Pericles had the slaves in mind when, in the first winter of the Peloponnesian war, he spoke in honour of the city of Athens for whom her sons had died. And what did the labyrinthine and costly protection of the law mean to families which scarcely knew where to turn for the next meal or the next instalment of the rent? Humble origins and stinted means did not prevent resolute, articulate, and outstandingly gifted men from seizing legal weapons and turning them successfully against their betters. But such men are always few.

For centuries, in fact, England had a legal system which alternately ignored and terrorized nine-tenths of the population; a system of local government dignified by modern writers as 'self-government at the king's command', whose exclusive rotarianism gave the propertied classes a licence to run the counties in their own interest; and a central government organized so as to per-petuate the privileges and ascendancy of the families that made it the arena in which they struggled for power and for the rich harvest of patronage upon which the successful contenders could feast.

At opportune moments the focus of political power broadened, as it did in the later Middle Ages and in the later years of the seventeenth century.[5] But the circumstances of those times were unusual; and a return to more normal times soon brought a narrowing of the focus and with it a return to the familiar order of things. Nineteenth-century reform deferred to the new realities of commercial and industrial power to the extent of admitting the middle classes to the spoils system and by legislating to make the new urban proletariat a more efficient instrument of economic growth. But the proportion of male adults eligible to vote after 1832 was not very different from what it had been in 1688; and

[5] A. R. Bridbury, *Economic Growth: England in the Late Middle Ages,* Allen & Unwin, 1962, *passim*; J. H. Plumb, 'The Growth of the Electorate in England from 1600 to 1715', *Past and Present,* no. 45, 1969, *passim.*

if population growth and rising incomes increased that proportion between 1832 and 1867, the operation of the Chandos
Clause, which enfranchised certain classes of tenants-at-will had
the effect of fortifying the landlords, on whom these tenants
depended, against any vexatious or disruptive tendencies which
might have emerged from such increases. Reform swept through
judiciary and civil service, the armed services and local government, but when it had done its work, considerations of wealth
and influence, birth and education, surviving all changes, continued to settle questions of preferment in politics and the
professions as they had done hitherto; and what is infinitely more
disquieting continued to exclude the majority from the benefits
that reform nominally extended to all.

And they did so because reform never tackled fundamental
problems seriously. Even franchise reform in the radical terms of
1867 and 1884 failed to drag fundamental social problems from
the shadows and establish them as the central issues of public
controversy. For most people ineradicable obstructions still
straddled every forward path, frustrating their effective participation in public life, depriving them of the most elementary protection that law can afford, and consequently robbing politics of
most of its meaning. Ignorance, illiteracy, long habits of sub-
servience, invincible distrust of government and of everything
done by established authorities even when it was plainly intended
for their good, fear of landlord and employer, a nagging preoccupation with health in a society in which the disablement or
death of the breadwinner could mean the workhouse for his
dependents, malnutrition, dread of the winter's cold, everlasting
and unremitting penury, debt, crowded homes, wretched surroundings, uncertainty about work, which might not always be
forthcoming, and anxiety about earnings, which with advancing
years could very well fall—these were the realities that made non-
sense of party politics and the constitutional triumphs immor-
talized in the history books.

To men and women caught in the toils of these perplexities
it meant nothing that the law protected their civil liberties as it
protected those of the highest in the land. Without means they
could have no protection. And in other respects the law was anything but impartial. 'The land law of England', wrote Dicey in

1905, 'remains the land law appropriate to an aristocratic state.'[6] And Dicey, who wrote in disapproval of what he found, could never be accused of headstrong radicalism. The law of master and servant, not reformed until 1875, punished offending employers, when they could be nailed, in civil actions for damages, and delinquent workmen in criminal prosecutions which might land the unfortunate men in gaol. The small debtor was similarly discriminated against as compared with the debtor who owed enough to avoid imprisonment by going bankrupt. Compensation for injuries sustained at work was so hard to come by that even when the law was substantially improved by the Act of 1897, a government committee reporting on its working in 1904 had to concede that 'the workman who has no organization to resort to for advice and assistance is comparatively helpless'.[7]

Such was the culmination of a thousand years of constitutional development. Successive nineteenth-century governments might address themselves intermittently to problems of public health, factory conditions, employment, education, and the like. But they could do little enough without compromising the freedom of action that was the precious heritage of those with money and power. And looking back on what they accomplished, as perspectives lengthen and the twentieth century draws to a close, it becomes harder than ever to see anything more exalted in their motivation than the ancient fear of tumult and insurrection that compelled medieval governments to control essential prices, and later governments to hammer out a systematic poor law policy. Consequently the working classes had no choice but to resort, for redress of grievance, to the unremitting pressure and informed advocacy of organizations which represented their interests. But the combination law governing the powers and, indeed, the very existence of trades unions, ranged all the way from gross injustice in 1800, to unparalleled favouritism in 1906, without at any time finding a reasonable status for working-class organizations within the law. Nor did the working classes have a corporate body with fund-raising powers to represent them politically until the

[6] *Law Quarterly Review*, 21, p. 239, cited by A. W. B. Simpson in *An Introduction to the History of the Land Law*, Oxford University Press, 1961, p. 260.
[7] Henry Pelling, *Popular Politics and Society in Late Victorian Britain*, Macmillan, 1968, p. 67.

Labour Party was founded in 1893, and the Trade Union Act of 1913 explicitly authorized union subscriptions to political organizations and for political purposes.

Political emancipation and personal freedom did not evolve naturally as a magnanimous legislature conceded the privileges reserved for the politically mature to an increasingly sophisticated and responsible working-class elecorate. Nor did they emerge from the clashes of parliamentary titans, as religious liberty emerged from the clashes of Catholic and Protestant dogmatisms. The constitutional historian, poring over his sacred texts, manipulating his precedents, immersed in his hagiography, has produced a comforting orthodoxy of doctrine in which evolution and conflict are blended so as to flatter national pride, and fortify all who seek an alliance with the past in canvassing their opiates and panaceas. But it is a doctrine as remote from reality as the spiritual logarithms of the medieval theologians, or the mathematical fantasies of the modern economist.

Before working-class men and women could enjoy any protection at law they had to be organized and educated and supplied with the means with which to dare to be the equals of their betters. And the law itself had to be changed, not only because of its anomalies and its grotesque class bias, but also because it knew no remedy for predicaments which were commonplace to the poor and yet incomprehensible to the rich. The struggle to achieve these things was made hard and long because the interests that resisted change were rich and powerful and entrenched. It was also made hard and long because the ideals of freedom and constitutional propriety, as understood by leading statesmen and jurists, lent themselves more readily to the defence of privilege against the inroads of egalitarianism than to the vindication of the great abstractions depicted in the history books.

Every tentative move to protect workmen from exploitation, to give them the right to associate together for industrial and political purposes, to make workplaces safer, to get the children out of the more dangerous and noxious occupations, to educate the illiterate and raise up the poor, was resisted, more or less successfully, for a very long time, in the name of freedom. And it was resisted by men whose forbears had used parliament, for centuries, to promote conspiracies in restraint of trade by means of Corn Laws and Bounties which had protected their cash crops; embargoes and tariffs which had kept out competitive imports; bans on emigration which had safeguarded their supplies of skilled labour; and an immensely complicated series of legislative enactments which had more or less successfully channelled the profits of colonial development their way.

The appeal to freedom was essentially an appeal to the spirit of the constitution. When Dicey turned to the question of social legislation, in his study of Law and Public Opinion, he expressed the belief that distrust of state interference had 'long prevailed in England'. In fact it had done nothing of the kind. If there were an attitude of mind which had long prevailed in England it was surely the attitude of mind that Adam Smith had castigated, the mercantilist attitude of unqualified approval of anything that the state could do to promote the interests of the landed and commercial classes, and to lend the authority of its sanction to the exclusive professional associations and restrictive combinations and agreements, by means of which these classes had facilitated their domination of the social and economic system.

Radical reformers knew better, therefore, than to appeal to triumphs and precedents of constitutional history which were so readily and disingenuously turned against them. Either they looked within, for the guidance of reason, as they had done in England ever since John Ball had flung his contemptuous challenge at the feudal magnates; or they looked abroad for inspiration, to the America of 1776, or to the France of 1789. Emancipation had to come by devious routes: by way of the formation of a mature, articulate, and thoughtful working-class intelligentsia; by way of the unsteady but progressive improvement of the material environment as industrialization spread its benefits to all classes of the community; and by way of the successful organization of working-class aspiration in clubs, co-operatives, trades unions, and a political party of which the Bible was not Locke but Paine, the prophet not Burke but Owen, and the methods were constitutional and not insurrectionary.

By the mid-nineteenth century working-class pressure had become both formidable and respectable enough to establish electoral reform as an issue of practical politics in terms which would have been not wholly displeasing to the Chartists. To the constitutional historian the Reform Acts of 1867 and 1884 were the triumphant fulfilment of centuries of development. From another point of view they were the first fruits of a grim struggle against the grain of constitutional principles, deeply held and long ascendant, which proclaimed that the country belonged to those who had a material stake in it. Long, toilsome, and frustrating years of campaigning lay ahead before constitutional thinking was unreservedly committed to the belief, finely expressed by Lord Acton,[8] that 'laws should be adapted to those who have the heaviest stake in the country, for whom misgovernment means not mortified pride or stinted luxury, but want and pain and degradation, and risk to their own lives and to their children's souls'.

But when, after agonizing vicissitudes, a political party dedicated to promoting the interests of the working classes did eventually return unchallengeably victorious from a general election, it did so by peddling an insidiously appealing political creed which sacrificed liberty to equality as shamelessly as its predecessors had sacrificed liberty to interests. And it did so at a critical period for parliament, when parliament was settling into a complacent and illustrious obsolescence, its quaint and antique ceremoniousness having been overwhelmed by the volume, complexity, range, and importance, of the things it had to do if government were to be representative, and the ordinary citizen were to be protected by its vigilance from encroachments upon his freedom.

In short the constitutional struggles of past centuries, so plausibly represented as a success story which culminates in the present, far from bequeathing to the community a precious heritage of freedom and representative government, have in fact done little more than deposit a heap of broken precedents and antiquated parliamentary machinery at its feet. Indeed the political emancipation of the working classes has fatally impaired the efficacy of the aristocratic institutions through which government must be seen to be working, without in the least affecting the exorbitant emotionalism with which they are regarded, their majestic inaccessibility to criticism, and their incorrigible resistance to fundamental reform.

At present the desire to respect individual freedom is strong enough to withstand some of the pressures exerted by welfare, planning, defence, and the authoritarian party structure which has evolved to cope with universal suffrage. Hence the widespread

[8] *The History of Freedom*, ed J. N. Figgis, Macmillan, 1909, p. xxix.

but muddled illusion that the achievements of popular heroes like Hampden and Wilkes, whatever they are supposed to have been, were institutionalized long ago, and that it is not individual effort or voluntary association but the system itself that protects us. At moments of high drama, or sensational scandal, parliament heightens the illusion by springing suddenly to life. But it is an illusion notwithstanding : dangerous because the institutions we have inherited are not capable of dealing with modern problems; and stultifying because it confirms the reassuring belief that institutions are proof against subversion.

In this respect the lessons of constitutional history contradict its teaching. Its teaching presents the story of constitutional development as if it were the story of the building of a mighty structure with deep foundations and strong walls. Its lessons show that there is no more permanence in a charter of liberties or a decision of the courts than there is in a treaty between nations or an agreement to respect the Geneva Conventions governing the conduct of war. Such things last as long as the interested parties want them to last, and remain strong enough and vigilant enough to make them last. The longer such things last the harder it may seem to change them. Tradition supervenes. 'The cake of custom' forms and hardens round the living tissue. But the lessons of constitutional history belie its teachings in this respect as in others. Nothing is more volatile than a tradition which ceases to reflect what powerful interests want. Kingship itself, despite its hallowed and consecrated role, never yet protected an English king, unpopular in circles which mattered, from assassination subsequently vindicated by his successor, judicial murder, dethronement by statute, banishment, violation of acknowledged rules of succession, even from temporary abolition of the rank and dignity of king. The future is not guaranteed by the past. Constitutional historians committed to the view that there is a lapidary quality about the triumphs of the past have much to answer for. Not content with having transmuted the base metal of constitutional history so that a tale of muddle and improvisation takes on the nobility and splendour of an edifying mythology, they foment the dangerously complacent illuson that we can best promote the values that we proclaim so eloquently by preserving constitutional forms which never served these values before and are not capable of doing so now.

c

2   The cult of nationalism

At the altar that other historians serve as acolytes, the political historian serves as high priest. The altar is raised by the votaries of success to the idolatry of nationalism. For nationalism is the ultimate form of success in history. It sanctifies the historian's passion for coherence and simplicity. It dignifies his tribal feelings. It vindicates his partiality for stability in public affairs. And it excuses an authoritarian streak in him which prefers to see power concentrated rather than dispersed.

In national development, the political historian commends the drive towards the frontiers as they are today, or perhaps as they would be if justice were done. In any contest between the centre and the regions, he supports the centre. He backs the kings of England against the feudatories; the kings of France against the duchies; the Hohenstauffen against the German princes. His heroes are the nation-builders: William the Conqueror, Henry II and Edward III; Louis XI and Louis XIV; Frederick the Great and Bismark. He burrows deep into the Middle Ages for rudimentary stirrings of national sentiment, and returns with absurd anachronisms and obtuse misapprehensions. Where he cannot quarry nationalistic tendencies from his researches, he fabricates a still wider unity, the unity of western civilization, and recalls with evident regret the splendours of a period when Europe was in thrall to a fiercely totalitarian theocracy. When nationalism overflows into imperialism the historian follows the flag. He is all for the Hohenstauffen empire; he cannot keep the tone of pride out of his account of the English colonization of France in the Middle Ages; he is so mesmerized by the achievements and personalities of Charles V, Louis XIV, and Napoleon as to be incapable of making a realistic assessment of the true costs of their disastrous eruptions into Europe; and he has not the least compunction in approving of the spread of Russian ascendancy over alien peoples, as Muscovy turned from kingdom to empire.

His duty may be to understand and explain rather than to praise or condemn. But he cannot dissemble his true feelings. The king who subdues and disarms faction, smashes rebellion, and extirpates potential adversaries, may very well crush liberty as he does so, destroy local independence, and suppress cultural and social diversity. But if he unifies and centralizes his kingdom, so that his writ runs unchallenged within its frontiers, then much, sometimes everything, is forgiven him. Not that forgiveness is a sentiment that the political historian often feels himself called upon to express. So intense is his addiction to nationalism, even in its most strenuous and insolent manifestations, that it scarcely ever occurs to him to lament the passing of lesser organisms, or to notice that their passing may have entailed a cultural or social loss. For him the absorption of Burgundy was a notable episode in the political evolution of modern France; the reduction by Castile of virtually the whole of the Iberian peninsula to its hegemony, except for Aragon and Portugal, and the subsequent union of the crowns of Aragon and Castile, were the thrilling indispensable preliminaries to Spain's 'Century of Greatness'; and the unification of Italy, if it achieved nothing else, at least threw up a technicolour hero and removed an anomaly from a world of burgeoning nationalism. He applauds the destruction of the confederate bid to secede from the American Union because it thwarted a treacherous attack upon the world's masterpiece of triumphant nationalism; and deplores the Age of the Princes because it ratified the mischievous triumph of decentralization and disunity over the monarchy at the expense of the national development of modern Germany.

The Swiss and the Dutch may have accomplished remarkable things within the limitations of federal constitutions which respected regional diversity. But neither Swiss nor Dutch, militarily formidable though they once were, have ever made the earth tremble and the skies darken as their glittering hosts thundered across the plains of Europe. And it is difficult to resist the conclusion that the political historian's infatuation with nationalism is, at bottom, an infatuation with military power.

The political historian does not despise the civil benefits of unification. On the contrary he makes much of them, commending unification for quelling anarchy, promoting law and order, extending the market, and simplifying administration : in every sphere of public life substituting rationality and homogeneity for whimsicality and multiplicity.

On these grounds, however, the case for unification to hard to sustain. It is easier to impute anarchy to a social system than to prove it. Absence of centralization is not tantamount to anarchy; nor is the persistence of executive institutions which are clumsy and ineffectual. Such things, indeed, are barriers to absolutism. Moreover, historians who love strong government naturally stress the subversive disorders, the paralysis of effort, the disruption of normal life, and the material losses, that occur when government appears to lose its grip upon affairs; and minimize the disorders and losses that very obviously go on even when, or indeed because, the authority of government is resolute and commanding. In English history the fifteenth century has always suffered from a notorious reputation for anarchy. But for the vast majority of the population living conditions were never better, and opportunities never greater. It is difficult to reconcile the reputation with the facts without concluding that a state of anarchy which permits so much well-being has a good deal to be said for it. The Dark Ages languish under similar disparagement. In the tumultuous centuries given over to barbarian settlement, historians deplore the shrinkage of the frontiers of social, economic, and political life, to the point at which they no longer extended beyond the boundaries of the innumerable estates where benighted communities sheltered from the environing chaos as the tools and victims of local potentates. Yet behind the much-publicized disorder can be discerned incontrovertible evidence that the great plains irrigated by Loire and Seine, by Rhine and Elbe, were emerging into the political life of Europe. Districts which had once been little more than military cantonments, regions where sparse communities had once led a gypsy life of subsistence husbandry by making temporary clearances in the encircling forest and scrub and moving on when the soil was spent, evolved in these centuries into centres of political power and cultural ascendancy, of which the empire of Charlemagne was the fleeting symbol. Revolutionary changes in farming methods made these developments possible. They were brought about by the unco-ordinated efforts of thousands of farmers living amidst the interminable wrangle and skirmish of a multiplicity of petty principalities and minor kingdoms. Anarchy, if it is to count as a factor in the argument for national unification, should be made of sterner stuff.[1]

The political historian, however, with his frank preference for strong men and centralized institutions refuses to believe that anything accomplished when government is weak cannot be bettered when government is strong. Indoctrinated in a tradition of political thought which is mainly totalitarian in persuasion, and is inspired by fear of violence, he finds in the legislative and administrative ordinances of the absolute monarch, and in the work of the outstanding men who served him, the same charm of simplicity and necessity as he finds in the work of the political theorists, and the same sense of the precariousness of things. Accordingly, his distrust of the muddle and indiscipline of political systems in which power is dispersed rather than concentrated, is profound; their ramshackle institutions and administrative improvisations are abhorrent to him. How can he believe that the desperately violent antagonisms that strong government never fails to generate are ever more damaging to society than the muddle and confusion it has suppressed? But the insurgency it provokes has to be put down; and the result is often a desert in which nothing grows. And when internal quarrels are held in suspension, how often is that only because the great leader has embarked upon the insensate foreign wars to which he is so irresistibly drawn! In either case the cure of strong government can prove to be much worse than the disease it was supposed to treat.

Other civil benefits of unification can very well turn out to be equally chimerical. Streamlining the administration, which means so much to the historian, may sometimes follow national unification. One government does duty for several; and duplicated functions can reasonably be eliminated. Since, however, it is usually more prudent to conciliate the influential members of the old order by finding them new jobs than to cashier them and let their grievances rankle, administration may become more efficient without costing less. Moreover, such are the ways of bureaucracy that savings on this score are unlikely even when there is no need to make jobs for illustrious supernumeraries. Nor is centralization always the incomparable instrument of executive control that it is made out to be. In the absence of modern methods of com-

[1] A. R. Bridbury, 'The Dark Ages', *Economic History Review*, second series, 22, no. 3, 1969.

munication, centralization will not work, except for extraordinary purposes. Even the most uncompromisingly autocratic rulers of the past could not govern their provinces without extensive delegation of powers. And delegation meant, in effect, the resurrection of local principalities disguised as administrative districts, and, hence, the perpetuation under different titles of all the scandals that centralization is credited with exorcizing. Burke's dictum that 'in large bodies the circulation of power must be less vigorous at the extremities' applied well beyond the frontiers of the Turkish Empire which he took as his example. It applied to Louis XIV's France where the complex symmetry of the administrative system masked a similar problem of control. And its truth has not been altogether invalidated by the advent of the radio and the aeroplane. From what we have all seen of the workings of modern totalitarian states it is clear that the problem of controlling regions and satellite powers, from a distance, can at times perplex contemporary politicians and administrators almost as much as it perplexed their predecessors.

As to the claim that national unification extends the market and thus increases the prosperity of the community, the evidence cannot afford it quite the support it needs. In France, despite comparatively early unification, serious internal obstacles to trade were not removed until the Revolution. In eastern Europe the growth of unitary states was accompanied by the spread of feudalism, to the detriment of market forces. And in Germany the Zollverein actually anticipated unification by a generation.

In fact, people are, at all times, perfectly capable of organizing themselves to surmount many of the obstacles to trade, by making reciprocal arrangements to neutralize tariffs, and by making a facility for mental arithmetic an indispensable part of the equipment of anyone who has to cope with local differences of weights and measures, and with disparities between the face and the intrinsic value of the coins he handles in the course of his work.[2] Consequently the record of what unification is purported to have achieved is, at best, an equivocal guide to its efficacy.

[2] The medieval *Statutes of the Realm* are so full of exhortations to respect the king's standards in these matters that the only reasonable conclusion to be drawn from them is that people got on perfectly well without his standards. Cf. P. T. Bauer and B. S. Yamey, *The Economics of Under-Developed Countries*, Cambridge University Press, 1957, p. 91 *et seq.*

The political historian, however, cannot bear to think that people are capable of doing without what is tantamount to benevolent despotism even when it lacks the trappings that went with that insidious creed. His own politics are based upon the assumption that they are. But the totalitarian cast of his professional thoughts prevents him from crediting the historical evidence of their infinite capacity for improvisation that lies before him in abundance. Naturally there are disabilities that people cannot overcome by any initiative of their own. And it is with these that unification can help, though it very well may not. But unification, in this respect as in others, is not without its costs. The unitary state, once consolidated, will infallibly pursue an energetic fiscal policy, in order to build up its military strength and then finance its costly wars, and this cannot fail to depress economic activities, or distort them, and thereby undo much of the good that unification may have done.

But the political historian is not to be disconcerted by objections such as these to his fervent devotion to nationalism. His devotion is proof against any scrutiny of nationalism which questions his assumption that a big, centralized, bureaucratically progressive political organization will generally create for its members an environment in which to go upon their lawful occasions, superior to anything that they or their forbears could have enjoyed before. And it is proof against doubt or criticism because the true object of that devotion is not the civil polity but the state militant, the state armed at all points for victorious war, its population numerous, its resources abundant, its armies trained, disciplined, and impatient for action, its wealth readily mobilized, and its citizens as amenable in peace as they are unflinching in war.

Wars have been won before now by small countries with everything to lose by defeat. But victory generally favours the big battalions; and the big battalions require the ample resources of the larger state. In the course of time, therefore, the smaller European polities have been absorbed by the greater ones; governments have centralized vital strategic functions; the executive has released itself from any constitutional restraints that may have survived from earlier days. And the political historian who welcomes these changes as a desirable progression thinks himself acquitted of any obligation to balance gains against losses in terms of life, liberty, and the pursuit of happiness.

The large unitary state may have been, for purposes of civil government, scarcely more than a loose confederation of semi-autonomous principalities. Its size may have been, if anything, inimical to the effectual discharge of its civil responsibilities. But the political historian is heedless of such considerations. Without a scrap of justification he takes it for granted that Kent was better governed by Henry V than by Æthelberht; that the duchies that fought the kings of France were fighting their own best interests as well as their destiny; and that the States of Germany could do nothing for their citizens that the Imperial government would not do better, whilst liberating them from the pettiness and follies, the tyranny, corruption, and shabby dealings, of provincial Jacks in office. And in successive instances of annexation and conquest, escheat and absorption, the political historian does not see the colonial burden, or the tax-collector's demands, or the recruiting sergeant's summonses : he sees only the accession of strength to the central authority and its significance as a prelude to empire.

And he does so because his criterion of successful government is, at bottom, a military and not a civil one. For him the military power of the state is the culminating expression and ultimate justification of nationalism. He may admire small and obscure nations for their resourceful handling of problems of race, language, and religion, which defeat the bigger nations. But he can spare them no more than a footnote or a marginal comment. His space is reserved for the big nations. Size, however, is not the only test. Many big nations drop right out of history for centuries at a time. The big nations that dominate his pages are the aggressive, truculent, and predatory ones, whose spectacular victories in the field are matched only by the brilliance of their diplomatic triumphs at the conference table. Indeed the political historian takes enormous pride in his ability to describe martial feats and portray glittering diplomatic occasions. They are his set pieces; and he devotes himself wholeheartedly to the business of trudging across old battlefields so as to get things right, and steeping himself in the gossip and fashions of his period, the better to be able to recall for his readers the modish splendours of the portentous gatherings at which victory was sealed by treaty.

Aggression may be a powerful instinct in man. And war may be its most sophisticated institutional expression. But the political historian is not content merely to record its irruptions and trace their origins and consequences. Nor is he satisfied with elucidating, so far as he can, the interesting problem of how war and its heroes struck contemporaries. He does more than record and elucidate : he admires, and esteems, and even idolizes.

From Charlemagne to Hitler successive empire-builders have drawn and redrawn the political map of Europe, obliterating landmarks, carrying their freight of starvation and disease, misery, hatred, and depravity, terror, bitterness and pain, first one way and then the other, across the blood-soaked plains of Europe, poisoning the minds and corrupting the souls of victors and vanquished alike, and bequeathing a legacy of tribulation which cancels out many times over the positive achievements that can be placed to their credit. And yet they have drawn into their wake, through the centuries, a throng of otherwise reasonable men, avid to explain and excuse, anxious to dwell rapturously upon the brilliant and lavish things they did, to make little of the odious and discreditable ones, and to assess the consequences of their careers with preposterously extravagant indulgence. These men, historians for the most part, have lent their influence to a view of life which raises the waging of successful war to a point at which it cannot fail to be seen by many as the climax of historic achievement; and discounts the costs of war, the dragooning of minorities, the suspension of political rights, the curtailment of personal liberty, the pouring away of the accumulated wealth of commerce and industry, the reckless sacrifice of the young, in such a way as to make them seem to be scarcely worth the bother of reckoning.

Historians who respond to the call of liberty, extol the virtues of the rule of law, and recognize the civilizing potentialities of democracy in its promise that government by discussion may eventually supersede government by violence and intimidation, are to be found taking successive generations of crowned delinquents and laurelled tyrants more or less at their own valuation and constructing the main themes of history round their trumpery and mischievous lives, and their diabolical adventures. Man the predator, organizing himself in large groups for the purposes of communal aggrandizement, is a tremendous fact of life. But man the social being, organizing himself in communities for mutual aid and comfort, struggling to control ancient tribal instincts that rage at the most trifling expressions of non-conformity, and struggling to sublimate aggressive instincts instead of venting them upon contumacious minorities or neighbouring communities, according to the opportunities and compulsions of the moment, is another fact of life, possibly even more tremendous. History cannot avoid telling more about strident movements than about silent ones; more about active, vociferous, and flamboyant people, than about reticent, unobtrusive, and taciturn ones. But historians are not committed either by conviction or experience to the view that the more commotion something makes the more important it is. Indeed, it may well be the case that 'the invisible, molecular . . . forces that work from individual to individual, stealing in through the crannies of the world like so many soft rootlets, or like the capillary oozing of water . . .' in which William James had such faith, have in fact counted for more in European history than all the ravening conquerors who have ever sprawled across the face of Europe, and all the inquisitorial governments which have ever made the private affairs of ordinary people their business.

Consequently it is neither beneath the dignity of their calling, nor out of keeping with their libertarian views, for western political historians to treat the brief interludes when parts of Europe have managed to conduct their political affairs in a civilized manner, with at least as much respect and care as they accord to the melodramatic episodes to which they are so obsessively addicted.

Historians justify their preoccupation with military affairs not only on the ground that war is one of the chief interests of mankind, but also on the ground that success in war is the necessary condition of the safety of the state. They may be disquieted by some of the more exuberant excesses committed ostensibly to preserve the integrity of national boundaries, or of dynastic complexes, which in fact no one had threatened. They may even concede that aggression, though it may be prostrate and demoralize its victims, often rouses them to retaliation; and that retaliation by provoking fresh antagonism is likely to launch adversaries upon a hopeless and interminable feud punctuated only by interludes of exhaustion between encounters. But they are in no doubt whatsoever that the salvation of the state is the condition of all the other benefits of society; that war is its ultimate guarantee; and that the costs of its military establishment are, very properly, the first call upon the resources of the state.

In what sense, however, is the salvation of the state a question of such moment? The nation-state grew by absorbing lesser organisms. These lesser organisms had their own integrity. Yet historians never deplore the extinction of kingdoms, and city-states, and principalities, which were swallowed up by the nation-state as it grew to full stature. On the contrary, they assume that annexation brought the citizens of such places within range of prospects which were inaccessible to them before, without depriving them of anything that they could possibly have valued in their former circumstances, particularly when annexation brought them into an immensely illustrious dynastic empire in mid-career, or integrated them, with others, into a nation on the eve of glorious military achievements.

At some point the disruption of smaller communities, apparently, ceases to be an invigorating and rewarding experience for their inhabitants. Once disruption falls short of annexation it diminishes instead of emancipating those who have been worsted. And when the prey is no longer something small which can be devoured, or reduced to tributary vassalage, or merely beaten, stripped, and abandoned, but is, instead, a well-matched adversary, not amenable to manipulation, then the issue can only be settled by a first-class war.

Historians see war between great powers as some sort of test of virility, and defeat in war, which is generally followed by a endless recrimination, widespread disaffection, and bankruptcy, as a symptom of grave social and political inadequacy. The Turkish Empire in retreat becomes the Sick Man of Europe; Spanish history after Philip II dwindles into a long lament over vanished glories; Scandinavia drops out of history after Gustavus Adolphus; central Europe, apart from Austria, and later Prussia, has much in common with the fifteenth-century members of parliament whom the author of *Mum and the Sothsegger* taunted for occupying space without substance, like nought in arithmetic;[3] and the Japanese, contemptible after their brushes with Perry, and ridiculous in Gilbert and Sullivan, commanded the respectful attention of historians only when they started winning wars by defeating Russia in 1905.

In short the test is success in its crudest and most blatant form. Greece may have succumbed to Rome, Persia to Islam, without exerting one whit less influence upon the social, political, and

[3] M. Day and R. Steel (eds), *Mum and the Sothsegger*, Early English Texts Society, original series, no. 199, 1936 (for 1934), p. 25.

intellectual life of the world after their loss of independence than
they had done before it. The great powers may have done themselves infinitely more harm by gratifying their destructive and
aggressive instincts than their enemies could ever have done them
by turning them into satellite or colonial dependencies. But the
political historian is unimpressed. He refuses to see the nation-
state as anything but the culminating masterpiece of political
evolution and its wars as anything but so many struggles for the
survival of the fittest.

Natural selection has dealt summarily before now with lords
of creation whose deficiencies have made them unfit to survive.
Political evolution may very well deal equally summarily with
the nation-state, scrapping it as a disastrous mistake, and starting
again, perhaps much lower down the line, in order to evolve
something very different. But the political historian, who makes
the ebullient nation-state the central feature of his investigations,
refuses to hedge his bets. And he fortifies his faith in the nation-
state by means of a specious equivocation which links success
with popularity and enables him to believe that the nation-state
could never have done so well if it had not embodied enduring
needs and expressed the authentic will of the people.

He is nothing if not consistent, and the widespread enthusiasm
for nationalism that he finds in the modern world he imputes
to Christianity in the medieval. At both periods unrelenting social
pressure and sedulous indoctrination playing upon ancient passions
and ancient fears did their utmost to enforce orthodoxy, and
later, to inculcate patriotism, as the highest ideals to which human
thought and conduct could aspire. The Catholic church
undoubtedly enjoyed a long ascendancy before it was discom-
fited; and nationalism is now tumultuously in flood. The historian
with his pedagogue's faith in the efficacy of teaching links the
methodical indoctrination with the outcome and concludes that
the drilling got results. But he reckons without the incorrigible
imperviousness of the human mind; the large indifference of the
mass of mankind to œcumenical issues; and its infinite capacity
for taking the dreams and speculations of the finest minds and
distorting them to the point of utter falsity by passing them
through the filter of starved or defective imaginations.

He depicts the Middle Ages as a period when the ordinary
man's religious conformity was refined and liberated by the

beneficent warmth radiated by the greatest Christian teachers. But was the ordinary European a Christian at all, in the Middle Ages, except in the sense that he accommodated his occult conjurations, his superstitions, his necromancy, his fetishism, his phantasmagorical fears and his quaint, wild, and often vicious hopes, unpurged and unreclaimed, to the doctrines and rituals, the disciplines and proprieties of the Christian church, as these were construed for him by generations of clergymen who scarcely knew more about such things than he did himself?[4]

Nationalism gets similar treatment. The political historian handles nationalism, both in its rudimentary form of devotion to monarchy, and in its later manifestations as the diffused worship of the state, with the confidence born of his conviction that it expressed popular will, harnessed instinctive loyalties, and gratified primordial needs. But was there more to nationalism, at least until recently, than the exploitation by opportunists of the potentialities of the political unit that economic developments had made possible? Did these men do more than bend the population at large to their will, as such men always have done, by taking advantage of its docility and torpor, imposing upon its slavery to usage once they have established what the usage was to be, and working upon its timidity, its bewilderment in the face of wider issues, its cringing and ingratiating posture towards violence and intimidation, its capacity for stoic resignation, and, withal, its immense resilience?

It is easy to see what the ruling classes got out of Church and State; and easy to see what Church and State meant to the retinues of administrators and servants of all degrees who made a living by serving them, down to the last man who had one or other of them to thank for his job. Every community has its misfits : its idle and aimless malcontents, its thwarted careerists,

[4] J. R. H. Moorman, *Church Life in England in the Thirteenth Century*, Cambridge University Press, 1945, chapter 8, *passim*. Dr Moorman's sympathetic account of what the ordinary clergyman understood of his faith in an extremely highly administered and relatively well-to-do region of Europe is not reassuring as to the average standards that prevailed either there or indeed anywhere else in Catholic Europe. A less sympathetic writer could easily have painted a darker picture. See also B. L. Manning, *The People's Faith in the Time of Wycliffe*, Cambridge University Press, 1919; and the exchange between Powicke and Coulton, in *History, 8* and *9*, 1924.

its rebuffed time-servers, its throngs of the unemployable and the alienated. Large organizations can more easily make room for them than small ones can. And to everyone who served them, Church and State offered more than work and pay : to the humble they offered pride in purpose and discipline; to the adventurous the spice of excitement and glamour; and to the ambitious the prospect of advancement, honours, and fame.

But what did ordinary people get out of it all? The consolations of religion? They scarcely knew what religion meant apart from tithes and nightmare visions of hell-fire. Pride of nationality? Until recently, over most of Europe, loyalties diminished by the square of their distance, personal loyalties counting for more than local ones, and local, or perhaps regional ones, counting for infinitely more than national ones. The State is now organized, powerful, and remorseless; opposition to it is scattered, fitful, and makeshift. Moreover treason and collaboration now carry the emotional weight that apostasy once had. Yet even today, when mass demonstrations of loyalty to the State and protestations of devotion to its leaders have the liturgical function of the Creed, stress soon starts cracks in the façade of unanimity that nations present to the world, and ordinary people are quick to see that in politics, as in personal matters, life, if it is to be tolerable, compels them to compromise.

Europe was paralysed by Germany's victories in 1940. When the world-conquerors irrupt into history they do so suddenly and overwhelmingly. The world offers what resistance it can, and then submits to its new master before it is in any condition to assess the consequences of what has happened. The emotions of that long summer and of the hard years that followed have all but evaporated, and historians are busy manufacturing a version of events which is subtly falsified by their knowledge of how things turned out in the end. At the time, however, when nationalism is supposed to have meant more to the peoples of Europe than it had ever done before, who can doubt but that Europe brooded over other courses of action and groped for other solutions to its problems than the heroic ones handed down to it in epic romances of redemption through sacrifice? At the end of the war central and eastern Europe threw off one colonizing power at the cost of being overrun by another. But the peoples of those afflicted regions have settled down under their new rulers much as they had done under former ones, partly because one tyranny is much like another, and tyranny is what most people are accustomed to, partly because government at a distance implies delegation, and delegation usually means that things go on much as they did before, and partly because people adapt themselves very quickly when their emotions are not deeply engaged.[5]

Like the religion it has superseded, and the new religion of socialism that it exploits for its own ends, nationalism has its prophets and its saints, its philosophers and its evangelists, its codes and its inexpiable sins. It even has its missionaries to carry its gospel to improbable environments oversea. Amongst its most zealous partisans it numbers the political historian who worships no other god than nationalism and fashions the past in its image. But in worshipping nationalism the political historian foments a bloodthirsty superstition instead of doing what he can to expose it, and thus makes it harder rather than easier for liberal values to prevail and for a way to be found to deliver the race from the threat of mass suicide. The worship of nationalism is his contribution to the *trahison des clercs*.[6]

---

[5] Nobody welcomes tyranny or poverty. Millions fled from Russian control. But people will always seize their chance of better things. Those who leave their country for ever, in order to do so, are not generally leaving their country for their country's good. Those who stay put may not be content. But that, too, is unlikely to be because they are tormented by their country's wrongs.

[6] The present fashion in politics is to believe that the historic problem of nationalism in Europe is being solved by the Treaty of Rome. This is, surely, a disastrous misreading of affairs. The Treaty of Rome may have been inspired by the conviction that the leading European powers must never again be allowed to tear the continent apart. But we live in an age of Super-Powers. And, in the event, the Treaty of Rome is much more likely to turn out to be Europe's answer to the challenge of the Super-Power, than to be simply an intelligent and civilized attempt to solve an ancient problem. The treaty of Rome, in this sense, is not the death of nationalism but its apotheosis. And our children, if they survive, will no doubt see the national histories of the countries that sign the Treaty written in the same terms as we now see the medieval history of Burgundy written, or the modern history of the German principalities before Bismarck. The larger issues of politics will be inter-continental instead of being mainly European. But the problem of nationalism will, in essence, remain; for the problem of nationalism is not one which can be solved merely by enlarging and fortifying the groups that contend with each other in the prevailing international anarchy.

3 Nationalism in economic history

The worship of nationalism, as distinct from the dispassionate analysis of nationalism as a focus of group behaviour, is not merely an idiosyncrasy of the political historian. It pervades all branches of historical study. Even economic history, the latest of historical disciplines, has not escaped its contaminating influence. Yet of all branches of history none fits less satisfactorily into the framework of nationalism. Interdependence of ideas, borrowings of technique, shared interests leading to common policies, bonds of kinship and class striking across formal boundaries—such things are familiar enough in the political and cultural affairs of nations. Indeed national development is often unintelligible without reference to factors and influences which transcend national frontiers. But in matters of commerce and industry there are times when it would be farcical to attempt to make the nation-state an autonomous field of study. Fundamental things are often inexplicable without reference to foreign markets, or foreign sources of raw materials, or to movements of capital and labour across frontiers. When industrial components enter into international trade, the very concept of the manufacturing unit defies sensible definition within the formalities of national divisions. Terms such as 'The Atlantic Economy' have to be invented so as to make sense of such international groupings.

All this, however, has not made the economic historian less susceptible than his colleagues to the disturbing allure of nationalism. His is simply a commercialized version of the theme. National unification is important to him not because it means centralized government, but because it means wider markets. Forward policies matter not because they are an earnest of empire or a guarantee of strategic advantage. They matter because they make raw material supplies safe, or make it possible to supplant rivals in lucrative markets. The economic historian prizes not territorial expansion but output; admires not administrative efficiency but economies of scale. In an age of number, when the things that are real are the things that can be counted, his criterion is numerical. Following dutifully on the heels of the economist, who is the high priest of the new realism, he struggles manfully to master the techniques that the economist devises with ever-increasing virtuosity, only to find that his painfully acquired skills are often too sophisticated for the records at his disposal, and are, in any case, rendered obsolete by later refinements of technique, as the economist impatiently casts aside yesterday's novelties for today's.

But his mastery of these techniques of counting, such as it is, the economic historian places unreservedly at the disposal of a higher loyalty than his loyalty to number, and that is his loyalty to the nation-state. It may be difficult to accommodate the workings of an economic system which is essentially international to the intellectual autarky of this intense preoccupation with the nation-state; but there is a sense in which the results of a multiplicity of factors can be summarized nationally for the sake of the kind of accounting that is dearest to the economic historian's heart. The truly successful nation from this point of view is the nation with the best record of growth. And by growth the economic historian means increasing aggregate national wealth brought about, usually, by installing ever more complex manufacturing techniques in larger and larger firms, and massing a soaring population in bigger and bigger towns.

Wealth does not mean leisure, or quiet, or a life free from strain or hurry. It does not mean pleasant surroundings at home or agreeable conditions at work. It does not mean a population big enough to make economic relationships as productive as specialization can make them without at the same time transforming social relationships from a fruitful intercourse into a fight against intolerable congestion. It does not even mean a decent standard of living for every member of the community. It means exactly what it says: the multiplication of goods and services, regardless of what these may be, produced without thought for social costs or political consequences, and distributed according to rules about claims which the economic historian does not presume to question.

Defined in this way, it is easy to see that the accelerated

D

accumulation of wealth is its own justification. In the absence of industrialization, when population increases more rapidly than land is turned over to the growing of food, large numbers of people starve to death or fall victim to deficiency diseases, as they did in England in the thirteenth and sixteenth centuries. Rents rise, however, profits increase, more wealth is produced than before, and economic historians are disposed to describe the situation, often in rhapsodic terms, as one of expansion and ebullience. On other occasions, when disease and starvation have restored some sort of balance between population and land, so that farming rents fall and farming profits dwindle because land is no longer scarce, as they did in the later Middle Ages, the economic historian writes glumly of recession and decay and imputes melancholy to the age. Perhaps he feels that the population, though well-fed instead of starved, ought to have felt as he does about the reduction in the total quantity of wealth produced when comparatively primitive techniques of farming were applied to fewer acres of land by a very much smaller number of people. People, however, have an incorrigible aversion to being depressed by the removal of the threat of starvation; consequently the historian's melancholy is exclusively his own.

Industrialization, with its electrifying effect upon the statistics, rouses the economic historian to hyperbolical enthusiasm. And the Industrial Revolution, which made England richer and more powerful than ever before, and for a brief span, richer and more powerful than any other nation on earth, heartens the patriot, as well as exciting the economist, in the English historian's breast. The Industrial Revolution, however, caused intense misery and transformed a nation of villagers into a nation of town-dwellers. And there was a time, before his infatuation with numbers drove every other consideration from his mind, when the economic historian could believe that the process of industrialization was a terrible ordeal, and that the benefits of industrialization, at that stage, were reserved mainly for employers, an aristocracy of well-paid workers, survivors, and those who were fortunate enough to be born when the worst was over. Today, orthodoxy prescribes a strict regimen of figures; the figures are in dispute; and so fragmentary is the evidence that they may never be agreed. But the economic historian will no longer countenance the possibility that unlocking the secret of cornucopia could have caused widespread distress; dismisses as tendentious the evidence that it might have done so, mainly because the scholars who stress it usually subscribe to unfashionable political creeds; and ignores a simple but fundamental objection to his somewhat brash confidence in the validity of the quantitative view of life : an objection which must be made to any attempt to quantify the differences between two utterly different ways of life and conclude from the figures that people were better or worse off for the change from one to the other. Living in towns may be perdition to countrymen because the work is abhorrent, the environment insupportable, and the hazards uncongenial. Banished to Arcadia, generations of townsmen have certainly found the compensations of health and affluence a poor exchange for the garish temptations and lavish splendours of the smart world they have left behind. The crucial factors are intangible, however, and it is beyond the power of statistics to measure them. Even if the quantifiable evidence were in fact good enough to establish an overwhelming advantage, in certain respects, one way or the other, the economic historian's unhesitating conviction would be difficult to justify. In the circumstances it is gratuitous.

People certainly flooded into the towns during the Industrial Revolution. But they may very well have been driven as well as attracted to them, for the Industrial Revolution was accompanied by a phenomenal growth of population. The growth was not simply an English problem. It was not even confined to the British Isles. The rising tide of population swept over the entire continent of Europe, as it had done so often before, setting problems of food supply in progressive countries which were hardly less acute than those it set in backward and sluggish ones. The economic historian, however, quick to seize an advantage, claims that industrialization, whatever it may have done to England socially, at least made it possible for England to keep its population alive. The claim is a curious one since industrialization diverted resources from agriculture, or at any rate absorbed resources which could have gone into agriculture, without substantially affecting the quality of food imported until long after Corn Law repeal, in 1846, opened the English market, permanently, to Russian and later to American grain.

By mid-century the worst problems created by industrialization were being tackled, and the condition of the people slowly improved. Thereafter industrialization brought the widespread benefits that the economic historian never tires of recounting. It was an utterly different world from the rural world of the eighteenth century. Intoxicated by the success of industrialization as a progenitor of material wealth, the economic historian insists that it was a better world, and treats with bantering contempt anyone, historian or otherwise, who regrets the passing of the old order. But is the case for welcoming this stupendous movement any better than the case for deploring it? And is it for the economic historian to make out a case for the contention that it was either a good or a bad thing? Industrialization was, doubtless, inevitable, given England's resources, political stability, and industrial and commercial past. And once it started to pay for the import of prodigious quantities of corn and meat, industrialization doubtless sustained a larger population than rural England could have done, and supplied it with a plenitude and variety of manufactured goods that were inconceivable under earlier industrial dispensations. But with success, in terms of measurable things, tilting the balance, the economic historian will not allow that a society which was poorer in material circumstances may have been compensated for its penury in other ways.

Moreover in assessing the costs of industrialization, he resolutely confines his attention to England, although one of the chief costs of English industrialization was incurred abroad. He will speak of the dank and crowded hovels in which the new industrial army had to live; he will remark upon such things as the insanitariness of the towns, the harsh and unwelcome discipline of factory life, and the horror and torment of urban unemployment in a society which had not foreseen the exigencies of the trade cycle. But on the subject of the traffic in human cattle on which depended the cotton supplies that fed the mills of Lancashire, he is, to say the least, reticent. Is this merely ordinary human fallibility: a failure to see old unhappy far-off things when they happen to have occurred in countries thousands of miles from England? Or is it something else?

'All nations', said Dwight Morrow, 'are prone to judge themselves by the loftiness of their own purposes, and to judge other nations by their failure to attain their high purposes.'[1] Historians are not exempt from this stricture, their partiality for nationalism

[1] H. Nicholson, *Dwight Morrow*, Constable, 1935, p. 281.

in general quickening into the most magnanimous interpretation of the actions of their fellow-countrymen, and passing over into recklessly uncritical claims, usually expressed with deceptively becoming sobriety, as to the priority of their fellow-countrymen in achievement, their instinctive sagacity in politics, their skill, their industry, their courage, their realism, their essential humanity, the radiant immortality of their heroes, and the sublime accomplishments of their artists, philosophers, and men of science. This partiality accounts perhaps for the persistence of the constitutional historian's belief, despite accumulating evidence to the contrary, that parliamentary institutions were the unique product of the medieval English genius for political innovation. It certainly accounts for the unspoken agreement, amounting to conspiracy, common to historians of all types, to ignore the Channel as a formative factor of transcendent importance in English life, and to ascribe the comparative tranquillity of English history, and its unmilitaristic tone, to flattering qualities in the English character, rather than to the gift of fortune that endowed England with the finest moat in Europe. Does it not also, perhaps, account for the economic historian's evident reluctance to recognize slavery and the slave trade as one of the outstanding costs of English industrialization? Is it not something more than a coincidence that it is mainly English historians who have shed a proud and sentimental tear over England's leadership in the abolition movement, and mainly foreign historians who have attempted to unravel the less than disinterested motives that may have lurked behind that leadership?[2]

It is true that slavery flourished before the age that could afford to be sentimental about women and children; and that at the time when merchants were plying their loathsome trade in human flesh, women and children were working in conditions of incredible hardship in their frowsty, tumble-down cottages, and in the early mines and factories. At that time, too, clan-chiefs were clearing the Highlands for sheep with no more compunction for their loyal clansmen than absentee English landlords were to show for the Irish peasants whom they cleared from their farms when tillage

---

[2] Eric Williams, *Capitalism and Slavery*, André Deutsch, 1964. A bitter book whose sweeping conclusions have not gone unchallenged. Cf. R. T. Anstey, 'Capitalism and Slavery: A Critique', *Economic History Review*, second series, *21*, no. 2, 1968.

rents fell in the years after Waterloo. But an impassable gulf divides the terrible rigours that necessity imposed upon the English poor, and even the appalling sufferings that rich landlords visited upon a superfluous tenantry, from the diabolical vileness of the traffic that created the wealth of Liverpool and consolidated the wealth of Bristol. Slavery did not start with cotton; nor is it certain that American slavery was languishing in the late eighteenth century, before the age of cotton. But it was the cotton gin and the Lancashire trade that gave it an unparalleled impetus, if not a fresh lease of life; and it is the Lancashire trade therefore, and the Industrial Revolution that it fed, that have a great deal more to answer for than the economic historian willingly allows for in his calculations.

When he turns to the prodigies of industrialization that followed in quick succession upon the pioneering achievements of Britain, the economic historian finds things even better ordered abroad than at home. One by one the leading nations of the modern world soon equalled and presently surpassed Britain in volume of output, in size of plant, and in concentration of industrial power. It gives the economic historian no comfort to reflect that two of Britain's statistical rivals, America and Russia, were not so much nations as sub-continental empires; and that the third, Germany, though smaller than they were, was nevertheless bigger than Britain, and better endowed with natural resources. Nor does it console him that these portentous accomplishments apparently did not bring improvements to American, Russian, or German standards of living, at least until 1914, which were as rapid as those that Britain's less sensational achievements brought to the standard of living of ordinary Englishmen, despite the lower and, apparently, flagging rate of industrial growth that economic historians unanimously deplore.[3]

What the economic historian really values is tangible evidence of national strength embodied in ostentatious concentrations of industrial plant, and expressed in financial statements which flaunt these unsurpassed prodigies of capitalization before a wondering and admiring world. In his eyes Britain was eclipsed and disparaged; and patriotic mortification at the triumphs of rival

[3] E. H. Phelps Brown and S. V. Hopkins, *The Course of Wage-Rates in Five Countries, 1860–1939*, Oxford Economic Papers, 1950.

economies is over-mastered by his passion for output and his respect for massive and controlled power.

Yet the very thing that commands his immoderate and un-critical approbation may very well have frustrated, or at any rate impeded, the purposes it was purported to serve. The vast capital structures, the integrated industries, the colossal interlocking empires of banking and finance, that so dazzle and bewitch him, were neither the necessary causes nor indeed the inevitable con-sequences of the apparently inexhaustible plenitude of goods and services that he depicts with such jealous but ardent emotion.

Left to themselves market forces will undoubtedly encourage some firms to grow bigger than others, and some industries to grow bigger than others. But left to themselves, market forces will only very rarely permit firms or industries to grow so big that they dominate the market and determine, within limits, what the consumer shall buy and at what price. In the last resort inter-national trade is the safeguard of consumer sovereignty. The fledgling giant, having eliminated all his local rivals, finds himself unable to exploit his local empire because its creation has attracted competition from abroad. But market forces are very rarely left to themselves. Indeed between 1860, when Gladstone virtually com-pleted the work of Huskisson and Peel, and 1932, when the Import Duties Act closed the era of free trade, Britain was the only nation on earth to allow market forces to mould its economic life almost entirely without benefit of subsidy, relief, protection, and other forms of preferential solicitude for native enterprise. Little or nothing was done to prolong the existence, or expand the scale, of commercial and industrial activities which market forces might otherwise have condemned, or to which they might other-wise have conceded only a moderate sufferance.

Market forces, even in Britain, did not operate in anything like perfect conditions. A thousand obstacles, social as well as economic, legislative as well as customary, impeded the movement of productive resources to points of maximum return; and social costs exceeded private in a multiplicity of activities in ways which government was either unable or unwilling to correct, with the result that the aggravating and noisome effects of very many economic processes were either paid for by the community instead of by the consumer, or were not paid for at all except in the health and well-being of everyone within range of them.

Elsewhere things were, in some respects, very different. If Britain stood at one extreme of the spectrum of intervention in economic affairs, by keeping government direction to a minimum, Russia stood at the other. And between these extremes it is possible to plot the positions taken up by the governments of other big countries, which intervened here but not there, or intervened everywhere but not as deeply as the government of Russia did and does.

The Russian case was, indeed, altogether exceptional. Military necessity, as determined by the Tsar and his advisors, dominated the economic development of late nineteenth-century Russia as it had dominated the economic development of Russia in the days of Peter the Great. Alexander III found Russia growing as naturally in its border regions as America had grown in its Atlantic provinces—growing, in fact, where commerce and industry had access to the skills, resources, and markets, of Europe. For military reasons he then forced Russia to grow in the less accessible areas of the heartland; and for military reasons forced Russia to provide for itself things that other countries could have provided far better and more cheaply.

The result was disastrous. The country was over-populated. It was desperately short of everything that was requisite for economic progress. Its social system was rigid, and patriarchal, as well as tyrannical, corrupt, decadent, and preposterously illiberal. What it needed from every point of view, military no less than economic and political, was an era of peaceful development of those sectors of the economy that were outside the immediate control of the government, and beyond the immediate surveillance of the land-owning aristocracy; an opportunity for farmers, merchants, and manufacturers, to respond freely to market forces at home and abroad, and by responding freely to create the wealth, the skills, the sense of accomplishment, and, perhaps, the independence of mind, upon which depends the civilized and enlightened tone of a society, as well as its defence, its political health, and its stability. What it got, however, was an unparalleled and incalculably costly diversion of resources from productive employment in ordinary humdrum occupations which paid wages, and yielded satisfactory returns to capital, into grandiose and flamboyant programmes of investment in heavy industry which never yielded anything like reasonable returns. These attracted foreign capital only because the State guaranteed investors against loss and paid dividends, out of taxation, which the investments themselves never earned and could never justify. In this way Russia achieved that perverse miracle of industrialization without economic growth which has been so recurrent a feature of her violent and distracted recent history.

The economic historian, however, is no more dismayed by the ruinous ineptitude of these experiments in centrally-planned development than he is gladdened by the visible evidence that contemporary experiments in *laissez-faire* were, by then, rapidly improving the material circumstances of most of the people of Britain. Russian industrial output rose sharply; British industrial output rose less sharply that it had done. Russia manufactured strategic materials such as steel in vast integrated plants comparable with the ones that Carnegie, with his utterly different structure of costs, was installing in Pennsylvania; Britain did not. Like his colleagues in other branches of history, the economic historian judges by results. When these are apparently brilliant and resounding he cannot speak of them without an uncontrollable impulse to rhapsodize. The price paid for victory in war, or for strenuous nationalism, or for rising output and splendid industrial equipment, may have been out of all proportion to the value of what was achieved. Contemporaries may have thought so and said so. And the achievement itself may have offended against his deepest political beliefs or symbolized the triumph of forces which were a denial of those beliefs. Nevertheless what succeeds commands his warmest approbation. And when he can see, in early successes, intimations of prodigious things to come, his approbation is unqualified. In the stupendous programmes of capital investment that Russia embarked upon so recklessly and prematurely, in the late nineteenth century, he sees the colossus of the mid-twentieth century laying the foundations of later power. And his prophetic insight works just as well with failure as with success. He sees the mid-twentieth-century tribulations of Britain in its failure, in the late nineteenth century, to anticipate the distant future by developing new industries beyond the point authorized by competition, and therefore, presumably, beyond the point at which they could earn their keep; and in its failure to do so at the expense of staple industries which were handsomely paying their way and earning the money that paid for the manifold material benefits that the people of Britain were beginning to enjoy.

The blundering follies committed by successive Russian governments are obscured by the meretricious glamour of subsequent Russian achievements, and ingeniously explained away by sophistical manipulation of the concepts of economic analysis. And the skilful competitive adaptation of resources to markets and costs that enriched Britain in the late nineteenth century, and enabled Britain to emerge from the world slump between the wars substantially enriched even by that, is discredited by Britain's subsequent failure to perform prodigies of growth in those international economic contests which, with football and the Olympic Games, now divide the allegiances and absorb the attention of participants and onlookers alike, the world over.

In other countries government intervention in economic affairs differed not so much in principle as in degree. And if diverting resources from activities in which a country enjoyed advantages of skill, or investment, or resources over its rivals, into other activities in which it enjoyed fewer, or even no such advantages, had less mischievous effects in other developing countries than it had in Russia, that was only because the gap between native and foreign enterprise was generally far narrower in most of those countries than it was in Russia.

The effects were nevertheless formidable. The nineteenth and early twentieth centuries witnessed what is probably the most extraordinary and dramatic accession of raw material and food supplies ever to take place in the history of mankind. Vast new continents were rapidly harnessed to the economy of international exchange. Some of the world's finest agricultural land was laid under contribution. Malthusian forebodings were suddenly confounded. Yet the considered response of the European powers with most to gain was that such benefactions as cheap cereals, cheap meat, cheap sugar, cheap wool, and cheap timber, must not be allowed to disrupt the social structure and impair the self-sufficiency of nations which needed strapping young peasants for the army; food and raw material supplies which were not at the mercy of blockade in time of war; and a population immobilized upon the land for the sake of the wealth and social ascendancy of a landowning aristocracy; or in order to banish the spectre of a radical urban mob from the preoccupations of ruling oligarchies;

or merely to gratify the farming interests. Accordingly every effort was made to prevent consumers from buying farm products in the cheapest market. A huge labour force was kept at work on the farms instead of being allowed to be attracted into industry. The rate of economic growth was deliberately checked. Political development was resolutely impeded. And countries in other parts of the world, which might have thriven upon European *laissez-faire*, were compelled to make do with the dregs of markets of which others were ordained to enjoy the cream.

And those who did get work in industry all too frequently found themselves diverted from the occupations in which they would have been most effective. Throughout Europe governments made prodigious efforts to foster industries which they deemed essential for reasons of prestige, or for military reasons, or for reasons connected with their need to foster or conciliate powerful manufacturing and financial interests. In their pursuit of these ends they bribed and cajoled, threatened and exhorted, flattered and tempted; they neglected no instrument of fiscal policy; shunned or disavowed no trick or manoeuvre of politics, no blandishment, equivocation, or subterfuge.

One of the most potent weapons was the tariff, whose nominal rates were usually high enough. But the real protection afforded by tariffs imposed upon manufactured goods was sometimes even greater than it appeared to be, owing to the fact that imports of raw materials which were needed in greater quantities than home producers could supply them, if they could supply them at all, generally paid low rates of duty, or came in duty-free. Many imported manufactured goods contained raw materials of this class. When they did so, they contained, in effect, a duty-free or a low-duty element. But they did not pay at a lower rate, or earn a drawback, for that reason. They paid the high nominal rate of duty upon their full value even though a part of their value was not liable to duty or liable only at a low rate. This enormously enhanced the effective rate of duty payable upon many types of manufactured goods, and consequently the protection afforded by the tariff.[4]

But the economic historian, who is ready enough to break into impassioned eulogy of any aspect of European development which

[4] C. L. Barber, 'Canadian Tariff Policy', *Canadian Journal of Economics*, *21*, no. 4, 1955, p. 523 *et seq.*

satisfies his addiction to size and his curiously selective devotion to statistics of output, does not castigate the governments that imposed upon the economy of Europe all the disabilities that national unification had apparently removed from lesser regions, to his intense gratification. He does not long for a greater Zollverein as he longed for national unification. He does not explain the comparatively slow growth of European real income by reference to those obstructions to the free movement of resources that figure so largely in his explanation of slow growth in earlier centuries. Europe's richest countries may have got where they are by investing their abundant savings in the productive technology of manufacturing and distribution that is the chief distinguishing feature of modern times. For this achievement the economic historian cannot praise them highly enough. But they have also retarded their own development and aggravated their own difficulties by imposing a vast structure of restraint upon the free flow of economic forces. In doing so they have stultified the growth of poorer countries by hampering their efforts to share in the rapid creation of new wealth, by way of the mechanism of international exchange, and by sharing in it to increase both the amount of wealth produced and its rate of production. For this achievement the economic historian has no word of criticism to offer.

What is this inconsistency of response but yet another demonstration of the abject homage that historians pay to militant and overwhelming power in the most highly evolved form it has so far achieved? Is this not the glorification of nationalism expressed in terms of the economic power upon which military and political power depend? Mere accumulation of material things has always taken a fairly low place in the hierarchy of human values. Generally speaking, what matters most, to people as to nations, is not to be as well off as possible but to be better off than rivals, or even to be no better off provided that there are compensations elsewhere. At all levels above the lowest, the pursuit of material wealth soon develops into a pursuit of means not ends. And when social and political ends are destructive of the independence and contemptuous of the values of others, Dr Johnson's remark, that a man is never more innocently employed than in making money, is a reminder that the world would often be better occupied in pursuing means than ends. The world, however, has always been murderously intent upon disputing the division of the spoils, treating production as a subsidiary, or even a fortuitous, matter. In such disputes the battle is to the strong. And in these disputes the economic historian is a dedicated spirit, freely indulging his partiality for size and power, confusing output with productivity, judging the welfare of whole communities by the prosperity of its employing classes, esteeming the large firm and the large nation more than the small, and devoutly believing that the quest for national ascendancy, provided that it is successful, justifies almost any denial of the ordinary calculus of cost. His methods of analysis are often wonderfully sophisticated; but, at bottom, is he not an unrepentant mercantilist, left over from another age?

4 Was foreign trade necessary?

A great deal of historical work may be done for no better reason than that records of certain activities were kept and happen to survive. But historians are not as constrained in the use they make of their records as they are in deciding which records to use. They are, moreover, free to bring to bear upon historical problems whatever assumptions about the morality or significance of past activities that they deem to be relevant or true. Like all historians, however, the economic historian is bound to know more about the rich than about the poor, more about those who wrote than about those who did not or could not write, and more about activities with which governments concerned themselves than about those in which they took no interest. And he is bound to know more about such people simply because the rich, the literate, and those who governed, had more to say for themselves than anyone else, or at any rate said their say in ways that left records which have endured. Consequently the groups that the economic historian can most readily investigate were conspicuous without necessarily being important, and successful, or at least methodical and assiduous, without necessarily having accomplished anything of moment. This insinuates a persistent bias into historical enquiry in favour of certain classes and certain activities to the detriment of all others, and by an inevitable equivocation persuades the historian that the fortunes of those whom he knows most about, and the progress of activities he understands best, are the ones that really matter.

Foreign trade, for example, has been a particular favourite as a field of historical study, for many years. Duties on foreign trade have always been energetically commended by advocates of policies variously designed to soak the foreigner, protect or foster native enterprise, relieve domestic tax burdens by penalizing the consumption of luxuries and trifles, or consult the convenience of those who assessed and collected taxes by authorizing taxes which were least trouble to administer. Accordingly, governments with a choice in the matter have generally preferred to tax foreign trade; and their preference has usually generated a spate of records. For the taxation of foreign trade throws up more than the fiscal records of liabilities imposed, and the legal records of debts unpaid. It touches a multiplicity of interests, foreign as well as native, affects the fortunes of all, profoundly alters the prospects of some, and produces a succession of petitions, representations, grants, disputes, and agreements, which swell the archives and impart an added prestige to historical studies of foreign trade by demonstrating the momentousness of the repercussions of government policy upon the political and diplomatic life of nations as well as upon their trading relationships. Furthermore foreign trade has the blessing of the economist who sees the classical theory of exchange vindicated as markets widen and nations specialize in the production of the commodities and the supply of the services in which they have some comparative advantage.

In short everything conspires to justify the lavish expenditure of thought and effort that has gone into the study of the history of foreign trade and to endorse the exceptional standing of foreign trade studies in the literature of economic history. The immortal glories of the English wool trade, sanctified by the Lord Chancellor enthroned upon a sack of wool; the spectacular revolution that turned England into an exporter of cloth; the fabulous saga of resourceful and ambitious merchants and intrepid sailors carrying English wares to remote markets and thus making their indispensable contribution to the industrial and commercial foundations of the nation that was to be the workshop of the world: these features of the story of English foreign trade 'as happy prologues to the swelling act of the imperial theme' have caught the imagination of successive generations and passed into the hallowed memory of the race.

But, as it stands, the story is suspiciously incomplete. It says much about exports and extraordinarily little about imports until high duties made smuggling glamorous and rescued the import trade from indecent oblivion by handing it over to the novelists and the musicians. It registers the fulminations of moralizing pamphleteers who denounced successive generations for squandering their substance upon fripperies from abroad; and spares a footnote, perhaps, for the findings of some laborious scholar who has painfully reconstructed the pattern of the imports of a few decades, or traced the fortunes of a single commodity over a longer period. Essentially, however, historians have been incurious as to the pattern and fluctuations of the import trade, which may be why comparatively little effort was devoted to that side of things until recent years. And yet without the imports, the story of foreign trade is not merely incomplete: in a crucial sense it is meaningless. For the purpose of exporting is to import. Exports are merely the currency with which a country buys what it wants. Earning that currency has always demanded prodigious exertions from the community. It has meant diverting into a multiplicity of other occupations, resources which were capable of supplying the necessities of life at periods when the overwhelming mass of the population lived starved and stunted lives for want of them. Sir Thomas More watching the wool farmers straining every faculty to produce raw material for the cloth export trade commented bitterly that sheep devoured men. But it was not only sheep which devoured men. Exporting goods and services has required the absorption of the material wealth of the country, and of its skills and talents, not merely in growing and manufacturing, not merely in ancillary services and industries such as merchanting, banking, and shipping, but also in promoting colonial enterprises at enormous cost, and in waging the ruinous wars to which they led.

The currency that took so much earning must needs serve some transcendent purpose if it is to justify the immense expenditure of effort that went into the winning of it. Yet economic historians are curiously indifferent as to costs and benefits in this wider sense. The pamphleteers they pore over were invariably concerned with balance of payments problems, when they were not railing at the immorality of wasting money upon the many worthless or injurious things that got in with the necessities that came from abroad, or warning of the danger of relying upon the import of supplies of materials which were vital for defence; and their preoccupations have apparently coloured the view that historians take. Like the pamphleteers the historians take the keenest interest in speculations as to the efficacy of policies which attempted to promote certain features of foreign trade, and argue, sometimes, as the pamphleteers sometimes did, that different policies, promoting some of the other features of foreign trade, or even, perhaps, leaving foreign trade altogether alone, might have done more good. But like the pamphleteers they take foreign trade very much for granted. It never occurs to them to ask themselves whether foreign trade did not cost far more than it was worth in the centuries before industrialization transformed it. Nor do they ever feel that their belief in the significance of foreign trade to the economy in those centuries requires some better justification than the magnificence of the records that survive for its study.

And so ardent is their devotion to exports, and to the splendid story of their expansion and diversification, that they appear to succumb to the error, of which they convict many of the pamphleteers, of supposing that the laying up of material treasure is in itself a sufficient end for a nation to pursue. Indeed they examine the volume of exports in such punctilious detail, and consider the terms upon which the corresponding imports were procured with such desultory attention, that the unwary reader may be forgiven if he comes to the conclusion that economic historians habitually confuse volume with value, and currency with purchasing power, and calculate the wealth generated by their precious exports, when they calculate it at all, without allowing for fluctuations in the cost of the commodities and services they bought.

That they are not immune from such aberrations has been demonstrated by Professor Imlah who has deprived English economic history of one of its most cherished truths by proving that the balance of payments surpluses of the first age of industrialization were not the tangible fruition of a spate of industrial goods, but that, on the contrary, they were created by shipping services, commissions, and income from foreign investments. He found that the visible balances were constantly in deficit during the early nineteenth century and that the error of supposing otherwise was due to the perfunctory nature of the work hitherto done on import prices.[1]

The terms upon which a nation can get its imports may very well be a small matter compared with the cost of being deprived of them altogether. It is not difficult to think of circumstances

[1] A. H. Imlah, *Economic Elements in the Pax Britannica,* Harvard University Press, 1958, p. 25.

E

in which the need for certain imports, which were essential to an economy, or imperative for the defence of a kingdom, or even perhaps indispensable to the maintenance of life itself, might have overridden every ordinary consideration of thrift. But the import trade of England, before the mid-nineteenth century, comprised a group of commodities of which only a small part was any of these things. Indeed the catalogue of imports for the sake of which wool was grown and cloth made, for which ships were built and slaves transported, for which nations quarrelled and bitter wars were fought, is one in which ridiculous ostentation contends for first place with frivolous self-indulgence. Wine and linens, dyes for the cloth-making industry, exotic textiles, spices and fruits, as well as an incredible miscellany of other luxuries, some manufactured, some not, dominated the import trade until the colonial period, when they were joined by sugar, and tobacco, and brandy, and by silk from the Mediterranean, and later, by tea and coffee.

It is not the business of those who inquire into general principles of social behaviour to moralize. The theory of value very properly treats the demand for all commodities alike, making no distinction between essential and inessential items of consumption, and assessing need by the simple test of what the consumer is willing to sacrifice for the sake of whatever it is that he fancies. The economic historian is, no doubt, perfectly entitled to examine foreign trade dispassionately, describing changes of pattern, explaining fluctuations and vicissitudes, and relating his findings as best he may to other aspects of contemporary economic life, without expressing his personal preferences in the matter. But the economic historian is not content, as a rule, merely to describe and explain : he marvels and rejoices when foreign trade prospers; he agonizes and laments when it suffers set-backs or goes into a decline. Once an economy is committed to a big investment in foreign trade, fluctuations in the size and prosperity of that trade can be very serious for all who are caught up in its fortunes. But historians who see men and women turning to other occupations when foreign trade declines, rarely express any satisfaction as other occupations profit at the expense of foreign trade. They deplore the losses without counting the gains. By this reckoning any foreign trade is better than none; any growth of foreign trade is better than none; and any development of foreign trade which can be construed as having contributed to industrialization needs no other justification, because industrialization to the economic historian is what heaven is to the priest.

This doctrine of the more the merrier could scarcely be further removed from scholarly impartiality. It discounts all costs except for the immediate costs of production and handling. It panders, without hesitation, to the whimsical eccentricities of the well-to-do for whom trifles from abroad provided a modest embellishment to lives whose simple daily round was dedicated to a routine of which the outstanding features were hunting, gambling, drinking, dressing up, going to law, building, intriguing for place, womanizing, and eating. It betrays its advocates into condoning the principles and passing over the excesses of colonial policy. And as so often in the writing of history, it ranges nation against nation in an idiotic race for primacy, in which the Italians take the lead from the Germans; then the Dutch from the Spanish and the Portuguese; and finally the English snatch the torch from the Dutch and outpace the French in the last spurt that carries them to industrialization and world power.

In their own defence, historians make large claims for foreign trade. They claim that it was a nursery of skills. It taught manufacturers how to produce for foreign markets. It taught merchants how to cope with foreign conditions. It created a merchant marine. It promoted the growth of monetary institutions. It gave employment to the labouring poor. It earned huge profits and channelled wealth into the hands of those who could make the most enterprising use of it.

The belief that foreign trade is a recondite skill which requires prolonged apprenticeship, dies hard. But it is not borne out by the facts. Writing of sixteenth-century techniques, R. H. Tawney once remarked that 'the machinery of international trade had reached a state of efficiency not noticeably inferior to that of three centuries later'.[2] Tawney could very well have extended the range of his generalization backwards into the Middle Ages when the Italians conducted their commercial affairs with comparable sophistication, and when even commonplace members of the English Staple could stand comparison, in point of technique,

[2] Thomas Wilson, *A Discourse upon Usury* (Introduction by R. H. Tawney), Bell, 1925, p. 62.

with their eighteenth-century Levant Company compatriots.[3]

If the complex business of mastering foreign exchange problems, handling factors, manipulating instruments of credit, arranging freights and insurances, grappling with regulations, and coping with all the other difficulties inseparable from the business of marketing products in countries very different from their own, did not prevent European merchants from becoming very skilful very quickly, manufacturers with the somewhat simpler task of making the right thing at the right price for the right market do not seem to have required a long probation before they too had perfected their methods. Medieval English cloth manufacturers were successfully selling the bulk of their output abroad within half a century of starting to compete seriously for foreign markets. And when their sixteenth-century descendants found that traditional qualities and traditional types of cloth would not answer to the opportunities afforded by sixteenth-century markets they swiftly borrowed ideas from abroad and adapted them to English circumstances and to the foreign markets that England served.

In fact one of the most astounding features of the history of foreign trade is the zestful alacrity with which merchants and manufacturers have responded to fresh opportunities by devising, or picking up, whatever expertise appeared to be called for, whether they lived in the dawning age of medieval international trade, as Europe emerged from the Dark Ages, or in the nineteenth century, when Japan, suddenly confronted—as a result of the Meiji Restoration—with unlimited prospects after two hundred years of virtually impenetrable commercial isolation from the outside world, quickly learnt what had to be known and then put it successfully into practice.

Borrowing has always had a bad name, presumably because of its disreputable association with the usurious grip that money-lenders have generally managed to fasten upon their victims and that the Church once tried in vain to loosen. But borrowing can take much of the stringency out of business development and

[3] Cf. Eileen Power and M. M. Postan (eds), *Studies in English Trade in the Fifteenth Century*, Routledge, 1933, chapter 2; with Ralph Davis, *Aleppo and Devonshire Square*, Macmillan, 1967; and even with H. D. Woodman, *King Cotton and His Retainers*, Kentucky University Press, 1968.

much of the risk and effort out of innovation particularly in poor countries where scarce resources are at stretch. Historians and economists who deprecate the commerce in ideas that enables even rich countries to benefit quickly and cheaply from discoveries successfully developed elsewhere are the spiritual heirs of the canonists who deprecated the commerce in money. Autarky may be no better an aim in business than it is in politics. But those who argue that foreign trade accumulated necessary skills and experience are surely committed to it. If they believe that foreign trade was its own justification, then they have no need to fortify their belief with further support. If, however, there is any doubt about foreign trade, then to the extent that its profits did not redound to the immediate welfare of the community, foreign trade merely taught lessons before they were needed, absorbed resources which had other uses, and compelled the country to learn from experience what it could have learnt painlessly enough from others when the time came for it to do so.

But foreign trade is defended by other arguments than these. In the early modern period foreign trade led to the creation of a merchant marine capable of withstanding the rigours of oceanic voyaging but not, without protection, the competition of the Dutch. Adam Smith thought well of the protection that successive governments extended to the shipping interests on the ground that it provided for the defence of the realm by keeping a fleet of ships in being. Defence is an unanswerable argument for maintaining a fleet. But defence is not an abstraction. It is not a comprehensive readiness to take on all comers, in all places, at all times. The defence of the British Isles is a different problem from the problem of imperial defence; and both problems are modified by the situation and circumstances of the likeliest enemies of the moment. Adam Smith's fleet was not the fleet that the defence of the British Isles required in the seventeenth and eighteenth centuries. It was the fleet that the defence of a colonial empire required. And Adam Smith's approval of the protection of the shipping interests, by failing to distinguish between these separate problems, runs into trouble by justifying one investment which did not satisfy his usual tests of economic efficiency on the ground that it helped to sustain another investment of whose economic and political respectability he was the most devastating contemporary critic.

Foreign trade is commonly said to have made for employment.

Employment has not always been what those at the receiving end have wanted. In the later Middle Ages, and in the century between the Restoration and the accession of George III, English social critics, observing the comparative well-being of the mass of people, invariably deplored it for the idleness it encouraged, and in the later period, urged that only want induced by populousness could make men work as they should do and once did. At other times finding work has often been a desperate problem. But foreign trade has not necessarily created more work than there might have been otherwise. The landed and professional classes whose caprices were the inspiration and for long the chief reward of foreign trade may have had their virtues; but thrift was never one of them. The money they spent so freely on imports would not have been saved if foreign trade had come to an end. It would have gone on other things; and the resources no longer committed to foreign trade would have been transferred eventually to the service and manufacturing industries created, or expanded, by this fresh accession of wants.

Foreign trade undoubtedly generated vast fortunes; and somehow it is difficult for historians to believe that wealth, particularly mercantile wealth, can fail to be socially and economically beneficial. But vast fortunes stir social ambitions. And the fortunes made by socially aggressive merchants out of the hard drinkers, the sugar and tobacco addicts, and the modish tailors' dummies of both sexes upon whom they battened, they then proceeded to pass on to the landowners who sold them their encumbered estates, and to the retinue of builders, decorators, and landscape-gardeners, the milliners, horse dealers, professional advisers and servants of all degrees, who preyed upon them as they had preyed upon their predecessors and would prey upon their successors. The gain to the community at large from this social mobility is hard to see.

As foreign trade expanded it supplied tobacco, and sugar and tea, at prices which were, in the end, within the reach of all. The historian is disposed to see nothing but good in this. And indeed the tobacco and the tea were an enduring solace. But the prices at which such commodities as these were sold did not reflect the costs that were incurred in developing and maintaining the foreign trade and the foreign interests of which they were the fruition. The real needs of those who bought these commodities because they were, more or less, theirs for the asking, were for food and shelter, and clothing. If they could have had the spending of all the resources that went to the production and handling of imports such as these, can we be so very sure that they would have preferred an investment in plantations, and colonial wars, and fleets of mighty merchantmen, to one that could reasonably have been expected to yield a dividend of bread, and meat, and cottages, and heated grates, and decent clothing? And if they could have had such things, would there have been quite the market of despairing souls that there was, for anyone with the wit to be able to distil gin?

Indeed it has generally been in providing for ordinary homely needs, such as these, that real economic progress has been made. Fundamental changes in farming, and manufacturing, and handling, have generally waited upon the development of markets for basic needs which transcended the boundaries of the parish and the narrow circle of middle- and upper-class demand. Concentrated into the hands of an oligarchy, wealth once inspired the engineering skills and evoked the prodigies of organization and enterprise that planted the pyramids in the sands of Egypt and set the cathedrals upon the plains of Europe. It provided farmers with the incentive to establish plantations run on factory lines in the classical age of Rome, and spurred manufacturers, then as at other times, to performing marvels of functional specialization in the making of lamps, mirrors, fine textiles, and the like. But which of these achievements has had much long-term influence upon economic development? The skills and techniques served their turn and then, like the monuments they raised, were one with Nineveh and Tyre.

Rome built a vast empire round an inland sea; gave it a common language; bestowed upon it the matchless benefits of Roman law; kept it at peace for long golden years; imposed uniform conditions of trade upon it; and fostered trade, whenever possible, by reducing customs and excise demands to a minimum. Were conditions for economic progress ever more favourable? Yet a potential market running into millions, served by cheap water transport, and presided over by the tremendous majesty of Rome, was not enough. The Roman world accomplished nothing of permanent value in technology and added nothing of permanent value to the common heritage of farming and manufacturing knowledge.

The Roman world was a rich world. But its wealth was concentrated. Immense landed estates created by laying every province of the empire under contribution, a colossal bureaucracy, and lavish patronage, gathered into the hands of an oligarchy the earnings of millions. The rents and the tribute paid for very much more than the enforcement of law and order, paid indeed for very much more law and order than those who rendered them required, and left them impoverished and consequently without the means with which to support an expanding market for simple farm and industrial products. The result was a world of grandiose accomplishment raised upon foundations of farming and industrial techniques which, in all important respects, were not very different from what they had been before the Romans had irrupted upon the Mediterranean scene.

The heavier soils of Europe which held the secret of European economic development locked in their moist and verdant slopes remained an unrecognized challenge until the oligarchs had departed. Then, in that obscure and disparaged period which historians call the Dark Ages, ordinary farmers, released from their bondage to Roman magnificence, with the disposal of their own resources at last in their own hands, had the means with which to live well, and the incentive, therefore, to experiment, to evolve new techniques, and to strike out into forest and marsh. The greatest farming revolution in modern European history took place not when sensational riches were being squandered upon vainglorious imperial pretensions, civic pomp, and flamboyant living, but when the rich were much less rich, when kingdoms were poor and ill-organized, and when ordinary peasants had resources to spare and enough confidence in the future to invest them in a colonizing movement of incalculable portent.

Once the rhythm of the medieval farming year had been established it persisted with extraordinarily little change until the later seventeenth century. From the English evidence it is reasonably clear that a substantial rise in the standards of living of large sections of the community, below the level of the middle classes, was signalized, at that period, by the increasingly widespread adoption of methods of suppressing the fallow and supplementing the winter feed of stock which enabled farmers to break decisively with the limitations of immemorial usage and meagre returns. Once again growing demand for basic things had exerted a tremendous and lastingly beneficial influence upon the productivity of those activities upon which everything else ultimately depends.[4]

The mechanism that transmutes growing demand into higher productivity rarely works twice in quite the same way. Growing demand may not induce farmers to increase their output or invest in methods which will give them an earlier start to the year, or better qualities, or yields. They may be perfectly content to be able to earn their living with less trouble than before. Buoyant prices and stable costs, however, are always a powerful incentive to them to increase output by turning more land over to the crops required and engaging more men to grow them. And farmers will generally be eager enough to adapt themselves and their routines to the exigencies of specialized crops when the returns promise to repay them satisfactorily. But fundamental changes in the techniques employed in raising the basic crops upon which the food and raw material supplies of the vast majority of people depend, have only come about when farmers with every commercial inducement to maintain or increase their output of such things have been forced by labour costs to cast about for ways in which to economize in their use of man-power. At times they have been able to do this, without raising rents against themselves, by increasing the amount of land that each man cared for, or by reducing the amount of care he gave to each piece of land. At times they have been able to go over to pasture farming, which uses comparatively little labour. As a rule it is not until these obvious economies have been exhausted that farmers look seriously for ways in which to use fewer men to do the work once done by a larger number, and stumble upon some new balance between land, labour, and capital, which henceforth decisively increases the productivity of those who are engaged in raising the basic farm products.

The crucial factor is labour. When labour is easy to come by, the market for ordinary farm and industrial products must be limited by the low remuneration paid to it. And the profits of farming which must, in these circumstances, accrue to land and

[4] A. H. John, 'Aspects of English Economic Growth', *Economica*, May, 1961. See also D. E. C. Eversley, 'The Home Market and Economic Growth 1750–1780', in E. L. Jones and G. E. Mingay (eds), *Land, Labour, and Population in the Industrial Revolution*, Arnold, 1967.

capital, are spent on other things. The pattern of the import trade into England, over many centuries, conveys some notion of what those things were. When labour is scarce the profits that accrue to land and capital are diminished by the premium that labour commands; but its earnings enormously improve the market for food, and clothing, and shelter, and warmth, and for the simpler services, and industrial products. And it is when labour is scarce that farmers are driven or encouraged to look for the kind of innovations that supply deficiencies in the quantity of labour, with spectacular effects upon productivity.

The late-seventeenth-century break with the past meant that in the absence of powerful countervailing forces, such as excessive population growth, farm prices would henceforth tend to fluctuate about a lower average level, compared with other prices, than they had done hitherto. Higher productivity, once farmers had adopted the improvements that were available, left them with reasonable profits even when prices were comparatively low; and lower farm prices left consumers with more money than ever for other things. The increasing pace at which everyday things could be sold to ordinary consumers stimulated the expansion of manufacturing capacity and presently inaugurated an era of technical progress. The terms of trade between farm products and manufactured goods which had swung in favour of manufactured goods for as long as these goods continued to be produced without benefit of cost-reducing innovation, shifted back and forth. Meanwhile population growth intervened once more as it had done, in much less favourable circumstances, in the thirteenth and sixteenth centuries. Informed contemporaries, like Malthus and Ricardo, feared the worst. But somehow a mass demand for the more homely products of farm and workshops survived the stringencies and vicissitudes, and carried England through the crises of the Napoleonic wars into the industrialized age when essential foodstuffs, bought cheaply abroad, solved the grave problem of rising numbers which had overwhelmed the country in earlier periods.

In this long story of crisis, and development, and change, what was foreign trade but an extravagant irrelevance which did little more than keep men busy working for the well-to-do? The sentiment that 'if there wasn't gentlefolks to make work for us to do how should we poor people get a living?' with which Mrs

Caddles attempted to silence her mutinous son in Wells's *Food of the Gods*, is one that may have been invoked to justify useless work throughout history, until Keynes outdid it by reflecting that digging holes in the ground and then filling them in would do just as well when jobs are hard to come by. But it scarcely justifies the unqualified approval with which historians endorse an immense diversion of resources into foreign trade when the farms of England desperately wanted for such things as barns in which crops would neither rot nor feed the rats, and systematic drainage which Caird thought one of the most productive forms of agricultural improvement.

With the growth of raw cotton imports to feed the new Lancashire industry the case for foreign trade improved, if we can ignore the plantations and the slavery upon which they depended. But it only improved to the extent that the cotton imported was retained for the manufacture of cloth which was not subsequently exported except to defray the cost of further imports of cotton. For the rest, the export of cotton goods, as of other things, simply enabled England to procure more of what had been imported before without compensating the community at large for its strenuous exertions by adding anything of substantial and general utility to the list of things bought abroad until corn took its place as a staple article of import. And even when it did, it is ironical to reflect that well into the 1870's more than half the farinacious imports, apart from wheat, went to the breweries and distilleries.

As to the re-export trade with which England held Europe to ransom for colonial produce as a result of her victories in the colonial wars, its protagonists have only been able to answer Tom Paine's contention that 'the expense of maintaining dominion more than absorbs the profits' of such trade, by ignoring it. The case for colonialism as a progenitor of economic growth, or at least as a powerful inducement to it, is very like the case for war as a challenge to commercial and industrial enterprise and a spur to technological progress. Historians seize upon the obvious benefits to certain industries and to certain interests and utterly disregard the losses of men and materials, and the wholesale diversion of resources from the normal business of life into occupations which were often more glamorous, or more impressive, or merely more clamorously articulate, than any of those that simply built homes, set up workshops, made the land productive, repaired roads, dredged waterways, maintained ordinary equipment, developed ordinary skills, devised better ways of doing necessary but unsensational things, and in a thousand nameless ways quietly promoted the economic development of the community instead of the imperial pretensions of the nation. 'The case for war as a stimulus to economic activity', wrote a distinguished student of eighteenth-century affairs, 'is, to say the least, unproven.'[5] No one could possibly make out a better case for colonialism.

The feeling that foreign trade has some alchemy with which to turn poor nations into rich ones draws its strength from the incontrovertible evidence of history that many trading nations have industrialized successfully and become very rich. But events which follow one another are not necessarily connected. Foreign trade with all the inescapable responsibilities and expenses that went with it doubtless added something of permanent value to the assets of the community. It would have been difficult, indeed, for so much activity to have added nothing. And with the social structure as it was it could be argued that any likely alternative investment of the resources that were absorbed by foreign trade would have done the community no more lasting good than the investment that was actually made. But these are deep waters. A country which had kept out of the race for colonial pre-dominance would presumably have kept out of war more often than England did. Ruling classes which were unable to fortify themselves with the profits of colonial ventures might have been able to look elsewhere for comparable gains; but without actually doing so their preponderance might have been the less. Moreover the very success of foreign trade created powerful interests whose implacable resistance to change, as the pace of economic development quickened, hindered the movement of resources and thus held up the real advancement of the community.

The foreign trade of England, until very recent times, has much to answer for. It did irreparable harm abroad and provided England with modest benefits at great expense. And historians who make much of it do so not as impartial observers appraising the economic significance of various commercial and industrial enterprises; they do so as the victims of an intellectual muddle which confuses the interests of planters, slavers, dealers in imported

[5] T. S. Ashton, *An Economic History of England: The Eighteenth Century*, Methuen, 1955, p. 127.

wares, manufacturers of exported products, purveyors of exported services, war contractors, and the like, with the interests of the community at large, and identifies the prosperity of the country with the successful prosecution of policies of aggressive economic nationalism without counting the cost to the community at which such policies were pursued.

5   The snare of central planning

The writing of history is an intensely respectable, intensely pro-
fessionalized occupation; and historians write with such reassuring
sobriety of tone, hesitate so learnedly before committing themselves to a point of view, and express themselves so circumspectly,
that anyone who presumes to impute to them a taste, sometimes
amounting to addiction, for melodrama and sensationalism, must
expect to be laughed at, and to have his imputations treated with
contempt. But the bending of high intelligence and sophisticated
techniques to trumpery and even to venal purposes is no strange
thing to a world which debases the miracles of technology to a
thousand worthless uses. Indeed the disparity between means
which embody the finest achievements of thought and skill and
ends which disgrace human dignity is a commonplace of the
literature of homily. And foreign trade is by no means an exceptional example of the economic historian's instinct for placing his
incomparable skills at the disposal of his overmastering passion
for anything grandiose.

His avowed political sympathies, his knowledge of the way of
the world, his training in economic theory, none of these things
is a match for his susceptibility to masterful and uncompromising
programmes of economic development along the lines first made
famous by Colbert; his weakness for commanding personalities in
business; and his extraordinary respect for sheer size.

He cannot see the makings of a national plan whether it was
devised in the France of Louis XIV or the Russia of Alexander
III without a lifting of the heart. Wherever he sees orderliness
being imposed upon muddle; national purposes absorbing and
redeeming the shabbiness and pettiness of the daily round; and a
grand design for development supplanting a congeries of lesser
designs; the economic historian cannot resist their appeal. The
orderliness may cripple or destroy valuable economic activities

which politicians and their advisers have had neither the wit to understand nor the experience to value; the national purposes may serve no higher end than the power of the state or the welfare of its ruling classes; and the grand design may be no more than a piece of impertinence perpetrated by men who have no more sense than to believe that business men need more encouragement to buy and sell than a cat needs to catch mice, and who presume to know better than they do how best to exploit the resources of the community and supply its markets. But the economic historian prates of reform and applauds the introduction of new industries and the protection of old ones when all the community ever needs is release from the burden of favoured interests and freedom to get on with the job of making and growing and buying and selling.

Everyone can see what a fool Alderman Cockayne was because his attempt to turn England overnight into a country which exported its cloth dyed and finished instead of raw was such a sensational fiasco. But no one denounces Witte, or the authors of the Méline Tariff, or the architects of German economic imperialism, in the terms that Adam Smith used against the mercantilists, though the harm they did their countries was more insidious and lasting. On the contrary, they get the benefit of any doubt there may be as to the wisdom or efficacy of their actions, and where appropriate, the most appreciative recognition of their success in sweeping away the debris of feudalism that littered the forward path to modernization.

Feudalism is consistently denigrated by historians whose reading in the subject is confined to the older text-books which distil the ancient legend that feudalism institutionalized torpor and organized the frustration of all the active and positive instincts of man. Nothing it seems can moderate their aversion from it. Evidence cannot move them. The technology of European farming may have been transformed, in feudal times, by new ploughs and more efficient methods of traction. They prefer to ignore it. They intone their lament that feudalism was inimical to commercial farming despite the medieval evidence that it perfectly suited the wine-grower and the wool-farmer, and the more modern evidence that it served the purposes of east European landlords growing corn for western markets, and Togukawa farmers whose immense contribution to Japanese development has only recently been recognized. In discussing feudal impediments to trade they disregard the extent to which medieval merchants met obstructions like tolls with privileges which liberated a great deal of trade from their influence, and take no account of modern observers who have found, in contemporary societies where such things as weights and measures are every bit as local and various as they were in medieval times, that traders, however humble and illiterate, quickly adapt to them and find them no encumbrance. Nor do they scruple to perpetuate Weber's disparagement of medieval capitalism, as elaborated and embellished by Tawney in a famous book,[1] when they might have dispelled any doubt as to the financial and commercial maturity of the medieval merchant classes, and the complexity of the division of labour achieved in medieval manufacturing, by reflecting upon the business done in the medieval cities of the Low Countries, the Baltic, and north Italy, as that now stands revealed by modern research.

Feudal restraints upon economic development, however attenuated in fact, were nevertheless real enough. And their removal no doubt did something to disencumber economies oppressed by market imperfections. It may be tempting to make large claims for the beneficial consequences of their removal. But it would be wrong to succumb to the temptation.

Until very recently, for example, it was scholarly orthodoxy to believe that Japanese farming output rose sensationally in the half-century following the abolition of feudalism by the Meiji régime and to explain the one mainly in terms of the other. It is now clear that the sensational record of Japanese farming in that period was something of an illusion fomented by artful peasants who made false returns to an administration which took a generation or so to learn how to beat them at this ancient game.[2] Japanese farming output certainly rose quickly : it managed to feed a rapidly growing population, apparently without sacrificing standards of nutrition, and at the same time supply the raw material for an entirely new and rapidly increasing silk export trade. And Japanese institutions were certainly changed by the new men who took over in 1868. Common sense would, perhaps, enjoin us to link the rising output with the institutional reforms were it not for the fact that Egypt managed to feed a rapidly

[1] R. H. Tawney, *Religion and the Rise of Capitalism*, Murray, 1926.

[2] J. I. Nakamura, *Agricultural Production and the Economic Development of Japan 1873–1922*, Harvard University Press, 1966.

growing population and supply a rapidly expanding world
demand for long-staple cotton, despite political weaknesses that
culminated in a legalized usurpation by foreign powers in 1882,
despite the widespread persistence of methods of cultivation which
had stood still for centuries, despite a *corvée* system which
probably persisted long after it was formally abolished by the
officers of the condominium; despite universal illiteracy; despite
methods of assessing and collecting taxes which authorized those
who were lucky enough to administer them to rob the peasantry
and pocket a substantial share of the proceeds; despite the
vexatious delays inseparable from doing business in nineteenth-
century Egypt; despite the monopolies and the corruption, the
bureaucratic muddle, the ignorance, the negligence, and the
disastrous experiments in enlightened despotism; and despite
the extraordinary fact that no one in Egypt had ever grown long-
staple cotton as a commercial crop before 1820.[3]

The Egyptian achievement was not brought about without
thought and organization and investment : irrigation works enormously extended the area of cultivation; new strains of seed
improved yields and qualities; foreign merchants came forward
to finance crops; and railways and harbours were built to carry
these crops expeditiously abroad. But it was brought about within the limitations of a quasi-feudal social structure which was not
markedly different in 1882, when the Anglo-French condominium
was established, from what it had been in the early decades of
the century when Mohammed 'Ali was Khedive. In this respect
Egypt was apparently very different from Japan where the Meiji
Restoration is said to have had profound social consequences. If
it did then the proof is not necessarily to be found in the Japanese
response to the market for rice and silk, since this was so strikingly
similar to the Egyptian response to the market for cereals and
cotton; a fact which bears out the somewhat otiose conclusion,
prompted by other nineteenth-century emancipations, whether
of slaves in America or of serfs in Russia, that there is more to
economic development than the abolition of the formalities of
constraint.

Historians who make much of these constraints and stress the
importance of rooting them out are never at a loss to justify the

[3] E. R. J. Owen, *Cotton and the Egyptian Economy 1820–1914*, Oxford
University Press, 1969.

F

utility of peremptory mandates, abolishing this and authorizing that, issued by central governments in a reforming mood. If reform succeeds, in the sense that economic growth can be seen to have followed in the wake of measures taken by enlightened and progressive rulers, then success is its own justification. If it does not, then at worst these rulers can be said to have performed a useful service in clearing the ground and preparing the way. Often enough, indeed, such rulers did a number of excellent things for the best of all possible reasons, as Joseph II did. There was no glamour in feudalism for those who had to endure its thraldom; and reforms which diminished its pressure did an immense amount of good. But reform was not always what it seemed to be. The terms upon which feudalism was wound up varied enormously, and sometimes left the peasant with financial obligations so heavy that he must have wondered, as perhaps he did in Russia, whether reform was not harder to endure than serfdom. Moreover reform almost invariably had the effect of increasing the power and authority of the central government. Historians are all too strongly predisposed to watch this happening with complacent satisfaction, and to deplore the irredentism which it sometimes provoked. Greater power and authority, however, were no sooner gained than used; and the economy over which they were exercised was presently forced to travel in directions it would not naturally take, and at a pace which it could not normally sustain. In this way, economic development by decree inaugurated a gigantic gamble, in which the stake-money was not simply the personal savings of the gambler and his friends, but a sizeable proportion of the community's resources, and the safeguard, not the insight of a reasonable cross-section of businessmen taking and backing different views of the prospects at issue, but the convictions of a small group of men who owed their power and influence to circumstances and qualities which did nothing to prepare them for the magnitude of the tasks they set themselves in presuming to remodel substantial parts of the economic system they controlled.

Where so much is uncertain a fresh mind can often work wonders. But its place is surely not at the centre where autocratic government can wreak so much damage because it wields so much power. Expertise in economic affairs may have little enough to commend it, but where the costs of failure are bound to be high because the investment is great, some previous familiarity with business must be a more appropriate asset than none.

What makes central planning such a costly gamble, however, is not simply that so much of it has been done without expert guidance. At the heart of the problem of making decisions about the future is an irreducible uncertainty about what the future may bring forth. The sensible way to cope with this kind of uncertainty is to spread the risks. In politics this means, wherever possible, substituting regionalism for central control. In economic affairs it means leaving the market to sort the shrewd and lucky guesses from those that must be disposed of by the bankruptcy courts.

Perverse fashion has it that anyone who advocates market control instead of central planning must be the dupe of the archaic and discredited notions of the classical economists with their odious indifference to the fortunes of those who go to the wall when government abdicates its civilizing functions. The classical economists are rightly seen to be the chief source of inspiration for those who distrust central planning. But the classical economists did not bombinate in a void. They witnessed experiments very like our own. The earliest of them wrote in the days of enlightened despotism; the last of them watched governments struggling with the social problems set by industrialization.

The classical economists certainly did not believe that government had no business with anything but defence and the enforcement of law and order. They did not believe that the market left to itself would provide for all society's needs. They knew perfectly well that some things would not be done if the government did not do them. They knew that the list of such things was a long one and included education, and public health, as well as the relief of poverty, the protection of children from industrial exploitation, and the care of those who were incapable of taking care of themselves. And they knew that business tends towards monopoly as surely as plants grow towards the sun. Their object was to advocate government intervention which would make competition between businesses effectual and do whatever had to be done to enable ordinary people to look after themselves. If business could not be made competitive then the classical economists were persuaded that the government must protect society from the untoward consequences of its undue power. If people were unable to fend for themselves then they believed that everything must be done to help them become self-reliant. Beyond that the classical economists would not go. They had no illusions about the benevolence or omniscience of government; and they did not trust in the ability of independence of mind, industry, and forethought, to survive indiscriminate largesse in the form of state welfare which takes the risk out of enterprise and deprives effort of incentive and reward.[4]

In the long history of social criticism there can have been few attacks more systematic, penetrating, and sustained, than those delivered by the classical economists upon the habit common to established governments everywhere of standing by their friends to the extent of protecting and fostering their economic interests to the detriment of everyone else's; preferring stability in economic affairs to change, except where change panders to national pride; promoting native enterprise even at the sacrifice of cheaper or better goods and services from abroad; yielding to strident and organized business clamour and ignoring the inarticulate and ineffectual resentment of the small man and the consumer until it begins to smoulder as riotous assembly or burst into insurrectionary flames; and enthroning the economic requirements of the nation in arms so high above all other considerations as to create interests which can then claim *raison d'état* for any swindle they care to perpetrate.

The classical economists called this frame of mind mercantilist and committed the tactical error of depicting it as a system of thought with a prophet, a creed, and a vogue at a particular period of history. For this they have been taken to task by historians who have not found it difficult to show that abstract precepts can never be systematically applied to the world of politics and that in fact practical politicians have never tried to apply them in this way, or if they tried, have rarely succeeded in doing so.

Disposing of an unwarrantable claim does not, however, entitle historians to treat the diagnosis of the classical economists as discredited. Yet historians rarely argue the case against mercantilist policies on economic grounds. They leave theoretical issues to the economists and take refuge from practical issues in the reflexion that it is anachronistic to apply the insights of the econo-

[4] L. Robbins, *The Theory of Economic Policy*, Macmillan, 1952.

mist to ages which were innocent of all knowledge of them. The economic case against mercantilism, however, is not that the mercantilists ought to have known better than to pursue such policies as they did, but that thanks to the work of the economists we now have a very clear notion of the kind of harm they did.

After yet another century of central planning can we honestly say that the history of central planning has falsified the beliefs and conclusions of the classical economists? A few countries are · incomparably richer today than any country has ever been in the history of the world; and central planning now has a tighter grip than ever upon public affairs even in those rich countries that explicitly disavow any faith in its efficacy. It is, perhaps, natural, though facile, to link the wealth with the planning and assume that the one has some vital connexion with the other. All the experience of past centuries is against it; but all the instincts of the present age are for it; and war, which has dominated so much of the political thinking of the twentieth century, seems to fortify its claims. When society is in gravest danger it is taken for granted that the disposition of its resources should be planned centrally. Wars, however, are not planned centrally because central planning is efficient. They are planned centrally because time presses. In war, time is not merely an important factor; it is the determining factor. Central planning gets results; but they have to be paid for in blunder and waste. Competition between businesses may indeed be a kind of war; and the urgency induced by competition no doubt carries its own freight of blunder and waste. But the losses are nothing like those that the economic system must sustain when grandiose state enterprises invest beyond the means of the community, or go wrong; and the threat to political freedom is infinitely less.

Meanwhile the old arguments for central planning have been refurbished. But they are the old arguments still, and modern experience has done little or nothing to add dignity or lustre to their antique but implausible charm. The best arguments for government intervention in the economic process and for central planning of economic affairs are still the arguments used by the classical economists. Keynesian methods of analysis and modern statistical techniques have certainly refined the controls with which governments are able to direct economic affairs. They have also made it possible for governments to tackle far more than they could ever have done in the past. But they have not made government intervention less mischievous, or sinister or demoralizing, than it ever was once it begins to trespass upon activities which should be left to individual initiative and private association.

Industrialization by transforming the material environment has been made the excuse for extending the scope and increasing the authority of government intervention. But the excuse is a specious one. Industrialization has not thrown up a swarm of new problems. What it has done is to set old problems in a new context and alter the scale of things unimaginably. Governments have undoubtedly needed different powers from the ones they had needed before; and different skills. But if they have used their novel powers and skills to do more than they once did, or attempted to do, that is not chiefly because there is more for them to do. It is chiefly because the temptation to encroach is perennial and irresistible and a formidable enemy and an insidious threat to political liberty.

Industrialization has taken people off the farms and away from the domestic system and driven them into factories planted in vast cities, thereby revolutionizing their lives, imposing new patterns of organization and behaviour upon politicians and electors, employers and workers, consumers and manufacturers, transforming the relationships between the sexes and the classes, disrupting the traditional religious framework, weakening traditional family ties, creating new conditions for culture and recreation, and generating new educational needs. The problems it has set are enormous. But they are not new. The nineteenth century was not the first age of the city. Cities had grappled with problems of water supply and waste disposal, of industrial nuisance and public health, of housing and poverty, of education and employment, even of what we now call town and country planning, when the banks of the Tiber were not yet colonized and even, perhaps, when the hill upon which the Acropolis stands was still untenanted. And if their problems were new not so much in substance as in scale, nineteenth-century governments could nevertheless call upon techniques of investigation and control which were new both in substance and in scale. Nineteenth-century technology which had set the problems also provided the means with which they could be tackled, if not solved.

And if nineteenth-century governments responded to the problems of industrialization by making them the excuse for wider powers and greater control; if they used welfare as a stick to beat the radicals with, as Bismarck did; if they protected heavy industry in the name of defence; nursed infant industries far beyond the stage of weaning; fostered monopoly under cover of the claim that they were keeping it within bounds; and prostrated themselves in humble duty before the farming interests; can we really believe that they did so because industrialization had thrust new problems at them? Historians have readily absolved the governments of industrialized nations from the censure that the classical economists levelled at their mercantilist predecessors. But governments have always expanded their powers to the limit of their opportunities and historians have always commended them for doing so. And it is hard to find much that is creditable in what they did.

At every turn, where they had a choice, the governments of industrializing countries took powers to do what people should have been left to do for themselves, and failed to take powers to do, or did belatedly, if at all, things that governments are rightly expected to do because they are the things that government is for. They failed to look after the poor. They neglected problems of public health until these problems threatened to overwhelm them. They did little or nothing for children who were in need of care and protection. Far from breaking the stranglehold of the professions they in fact authorized the professions to maintain and increase their remorseless grip upon the community. And they made defence their excuse for an indefinite extension of their control. Defence needs have always meant eating fish for the sake of the navy and tolerating dear bread for the sake of the infantry, or at any rate doing something equivalent in their interest. They have often meant building roads for military reasons rather than for commercial ones, and they have usually meant keeping an anxious eye on timber stocks and iron and steel capacity. In the nineteenth century defence needs become infinitely more complex. And amongst other things they involved governments in the business of building railways which could never hope to earn a profit.

Governments were rarely content merely to supplement private initiative in this matter. Sometimes they planned the entire railway system and built some of it, leaving the rest to private contractors; sometimes they planned only the trunk lines and left the rest of the planning and all or most of the building to commercial interests. There were endless variations. Ultimately, however, in most countries, they bought out all the private interests and turned the railways into a state enterprise. Only two things were rare : one was to leave the whole operation to the private speculator; the other was to refrain from following the fashion for nationalizing the system once it was complete, or later, when it was in trouble with the motor-car and the lorry.

Historians are, apparently, unwilling to see any harm in all this. Indeed the political and economic implications of government participation and control give them no qualms. They are innocently delighted when the railways annihilate the geographical obstacles to nation-building, and hasten the unification of modern Germany, modern Russia, and modern America. And such is their faith in central planning, and their admiration for the splendid simplicity of the denouement, when the state became the sole executive authority for the railways, that they are heedless of the fateful consequences of committing ever more power to the keeping of the politicians, and of strengthening the railway interest by making it easier than it might otherwise have been for the railways to bring clandestine pressure to bear at the centre of things. They are no less heedless of the consequences for efficiency of this usurpation of the sovereignty of the market. Planning the railways instead of letting them develop piecemeal was bound to be wasteful. Deciding where railways should go was not something that could have been done at the start. When mistakes were made by private companies bankruptcy disposed of them. When mistakes were made by the state, subventions and preferences concealed them. Deciding the balance between different forms of transport is also something that could not possibly have been settled when railways were in their infancy, or indeed settled permanently at any time. Yet railway policy was allowed to nullify the advantages of water transport here, restrict the growing opportunities for road transport there, starve certain industries or certain regions, lavish uncovenanted advantages on others, frustrate or delay changes everywhere, and induce an attitude of mind in railwaymen in which smartness and the punctilious discharge of routine duties did service for that efficiency which, in a well-conducted organization, is not only a question of doing the job properly but is also a question of doing the job that ought to be done.

Market sovereignty, however, was not usurped only when the state planned and later took over the railway system. It was also usurped when the state failed to prevent private railway monopolies from forming. In railway matters monopoly is exonerated by historians when it is state monopoly. When it is private monopoly, as it was in America, where comment was free to the point of scurrility, they are less sure. They denounce the conspiracies against the public interest and the corruption of which they are so fully informed, and condemn the wastes of competition of which spectacular and sometimes widespread bankruptcy was the incontrovertible evidence. But bankruptcy was not necessarily a sign that the economic system was working badly. It was often a sign that the economic system was working well. And monopoly was far from being inevitable. Standardization did not require it : remarkable things were accomplished in standardizing track, rolling-stock, signalling, and the like, and in co-ordinating timetables, and services, without benefit of trust or cartel. Nor did investment require it. The building and running of a railway was a huge undertaking and hence an immense risk. But it need not have been the risk that it was. The parliamentary legislation that incorporated the first railway companies envisaged the railway as a kind of turnpike to be built by contractors who would recover their investment by charging a rate for its use to all who had rolling-stock suitable for its tracks. Lardner predicted disaster for any attempt to separate the railway functions, and hence the business risks, in this way.[5] But Lardner himself was much impressed by the success of the clearing-house system, which presumably could have been extended so as to operate a market for track space comparable with the market for freight space that the Baltic exchange was soon to become famous for. And rolling-stock owned by the user was at one time a not inconsiderable element in English railway freight-carrying capacity.

The real failure in railway policy was in fact a failure of politics. Discerning minds were quick to perceive the potential dangers when railways were still a novelty. Within fifteen years of

[5] Dionysius Lardner, *Railway Economy* (1850), reprinted by David & Charles, 1968, p. 421.

Stephenson's 'Rocket' the youthful Gladstone had got parliament to equip itself with reserve powers against the day when railway companies might cease to compete and start to conspire. And historians who fulminate against the private monopolists or see railway monopolies as inevitable would do well to reflect upon how much harm could have been averted if the state had acted vigorously to check the formation of monopolies rather than belatedly to institutionalize the results of its own vacillation, laxity, and incompetence.

Other pretexts for state intervention in the normal running of the economy, as patron or sponsor rather than as guardian of the liberty of the subject, were scarcely more reputable. The case for protecting infant industries from the competition of mature foreign giants had nothing better to recommend it than a foolish misunderstanding of Adam Smith which Friedrich List embodied in his advocacy of it. In the mawkish atmosphere of gathering nationalism that afflicted the industrializing countries of the nineteenth century, however, List's arguments found a susceptible public in a receptive mood.[6] New firms may have grown to maturity in the United States, in the course of the nineteenth century, despite competition from established ones in other parts of the Union; and practically every other industrializing power may have had similar experiences, within its own frontiers, of infant firms withstanding all the efforts of adult competitors to smother them, despite their advantages of size and priority, because the late entrants brought a fresh approach to the raw material, structural, or marketing problems of their industry. But the campaign for protection appealed to tribal cravings and gratified widespread industrial interests; for protection, once conceded, meant shelter for all. It was therefore proof against reason and experience, even very recent experience.

When the chief European powers, in a mood of unwonted liberalism, relaxed their tutelary watch over the commercial and industrial activities of their citizens and, in mid-century, permitted what was tantamount to free trade, the results astounded even the most convinced protectionists. 'All nations', declared a recent authority, 'saw their volume of exports grow. Home industries did not collapse before British competition, but rather changed

[6] F. List, *The National System of Political Economy*, Longman, 1885, reprinted by Augustus M. Kelly, New York, 1966.

and grew stronger in the process. Marginally inefficient firms, vegetating in the shelter of protective duties, were compelled to re-tool or close.'[7] The mood was a fleeting one, however, and quickly overcome and forgotten: there were more imperious interests to propitiate than the consumer, and more urgent political ambitions to serve than the modest one of living at peace with neighbours. The world was moving towards its twentieth-century Götterdämmerung with its two lacerating general wars separated by a blighted interlude compounded chiefly of prostration, re-armament, and the resurrection of wholesale massacre as an instrument of domestic policy.

Historians who profess to believe in political liberty and proclaim their abhorrence of monopoly in all its forms are curiously reluctant to censure, though they are ready enough to condone, policies which sacrificed the political independence of the ordinary citizen, the standard of living of the ordinary consumer, and the long-term economic efficiency of the community, to militarism, prestige, and the trappings rather than the substance of modernity. So many thriving industrial nations have protected so many of their economic activities for so long that it is perhaps hard to believe that protection is a dangerous weapon. And there are plenty of contemporary commentators who see in the technological achievements of modern Russia and the economic resurgence of post-war western Europe a justification for central planning and assisted growth that Britain would do well to take seriously. Yet in the complex interaction of things are they right to assume a connexion between protection and growth, or central planning and growth, simply because these things are often to be found together?

The presumption is against them. Protection is a rich culture for monopoly. And once protection has disabled or eliminated foreign competition what is there to prevent domestic profit margins from being raised? With higher profits guaranteed, the incentive to do much with little soon goes out of business. But resources which might have served the economy elsewhere are immobilized by

[7] D. S. Landes, 'Technological Change and Development in Western Europe', *Cambridge Economic History of Europe,* vol. 6, Cambridge University Press, 1965, chapter 5, p. 429. See also K. D. Barkin, *The Controversy over German Industrialization, 1890–1902,* Chicago University Press, 1970.

the attractive returns; and investments are drawn in which in different circumstances would have gone into other activities. Moreover protection is rarely the end of the matter. There is generally a larger purpose, a grand design, to explain and vindicate protection; and the gratuitous benefactions it confers are usually fortified, in the end, by other tokens of good-will. The result is often splendid to behold : colossal plants, the latest equipment, glittering research facilities, sophisticated management techniques, and admirable welfare services. But what is not so clear is the net gain to the community. Higher prices mean lower real incomes. Fomenting monopoly means concentrating political power instead of diffusing it.

The ordinary calls upon government do not normally require that special treatment be accorded to selected economic activities. Defence needs, it is true, stand at every politician's elbow, to be slighted or neglected at his peril. And there are certain industries best run as utilities because rivalry between competing firms is more troublesome to sustain than its alternative. Everything else in the way of special treatment is either a disreputable concession to pressure or a witness to the deep conviction, shared by public men everywhere, that a statesmanlike view of things must reveal better than the market can the most efficacious way of organizing the resources of the community. Containing pressures rather than succumbing to them is a test of the fitness of the political institutions of a society. But the blandishments of the statesmanlike view of things beguile even the most watchful politicians with a thousand sophistries, only to betray them into the most egregious blunders.

Politicians are easily tempted. Power estranges a man from his fellows. It is a sort of loneliness; and man is a social animal. The man of power lives, therefore, very much against the grain of things. This is a testing experience. The loneliness searches his character, revealing his strength, exploring his weaknesses. And success then consummates the investigation. In moderation, success may very well act impartially upon qualities and defects alike, enriching and mellowing the one, coarsening and hardening the other; making one sort of man more moderate and conciliatory, and another sort more relentlessly uncompromising, arrogant, rancorous, and brutal. Soon enough, however, success begins to corrode the reasonable, sceptical, self-depreciatory controls, which normally keep the personality in balance, and sweeps its victim by way of derangement to paranoia, and on to a preordained climax of crime, and terror, agony, despair, and ruin.

Ordinary politicians do not need to have pursued this fatal course for long before they encounter the chimera of economic stability. As a policy stabilization has the practical political advantage of being popular in many very different quarters. It has the technocrat's blessing because it minimizes interruptions to the smooth flow of production. It is a benediction to the businessman. It mollifies the labour leader. It draws some of the venom and urgency out of politics. And it appeals to universal frailties which crave to turn discriminating respect for established ways of doing things into uncritical veneration for them; frailties which would transform insurance from a hedge against risk into a refuge from change; and which persistently invest the prevailing pattern of trade and industry with immortal significance, so that timeless verities are impugned if the world buys English cloth instead of Flemish; if it banks its money at Antwerp instead of at Florence; if it takes its business from Venice to Leghorn; if it drinks coffee, and tea, rather than beer, and wine, and spirits; if it wears cotton instead of wool, or man-made fibres instead of either; if its cloth is not woven in Lancashire, its coal is not mined in South Wales, and its ships are not built on Clyde and Tyne.

But in large doses stability has fatal drawbacks. There is very little scope for growth without change; and none for change without risk. Moreover change and risk are more than necessary evils. They expose established organizations to importunate rivals, which helps to keep them keen and active, and thus protects the consumer from conspiracies of business and labour, and the private citizen from dangerous threats to political liberty.

Politicians have a way of seeing the risks of change more clearly than the dangers and costs of leaving things as they are. This predisposes them to see the impending dissolution of society in every radical project and the disintegration of the economy in every structural change in commerce or industry. Historians because they observe the past mainly from the point of view of established authorities, whose records are often their only guide, are predisposed to see anarchy in every civil disturbance and comprehensive misfortune in every vicissitude of business. Stability therefore appeals strongly to both politicians and historians. Historians, however, require something more than stability of an age before their devotion to it can be wholehearted. It must stand out. When it does it inspires the highest praise that historians can bestow. It becomes a golden age. When it passes, as in the end it must, no one regrets its loss more eloquently than the historian does. Consequently a very great deal of historical writing is a compound of rhapsody and nostalgia.

But historians cannot bear to see success turn sour. When established organizations are eclipsed they turn, not without a pang, to adore the new star ascendant in another quarter of the firmament. And history, no longer a seamless web, becomes instead a patchwork quilt : a thing of forsaken themes, unfinished portraits, abrupt transitions, fragmentary views, curtailments, foreshortenings, abridgements, and silences. Greece has no history after the rise of Rome; Islam is a forgotten episode once expansion ceases; and what became of Italy after the Renaissance or of Spain after the Armada? Was there no Baltic economy after the days of the Hanseatic League; and did the Low Countries subside into the North Sea once Britain had settled her quarrels with the Dutch? The great cities have had no more luck than the great nations : Athens, Rome, Constantinople, Alexandria, Venice, Florence, Paris, Vienna, have all made their entrances with a flourish, only to be hustled unceremoniously away for a period of suspended animation until they are required again. And beyond, in outer darkness, brood the alien cultures, uncomprehended and, until recently, totally ignored.

Historians who cherish a view of history which turns history into a series of portraits of society at moments of stability and brilliance naturally abominate periods of transition. Change is tolerable to them only because out of travail emerges a fresh and radiant equilibrium. Transitional periods trail associations of violence and subversion and do so, partly because those in power keep better records than those who threaten them; partly because 'if treason prosper, none dare call it treason', and the records tell a story which has been suitably expurgated or amended; and partly because it is not customary to set the toll taken by civil disorder in periods of transition against the toll taken in stable periods by way of judicial or otherwise authorized violence and by way of other kinds of pressure, often deviously exerted. But there is much to be said for periods of transition. The discomfiture of prevailing orthodoxies, the collapse of entrenched institutions, the disintegration of ruling cliques and factions through irreconcilable mutual antipathies, emancipate men and classes, release energies, and liberate minds. All too soon they are over. New orthodoxies replace old ones; new institutions enforce them; new ruling groups oppress minorities and crush dissent. Stability is restored.

Stability can indeed be as remorseless an enemy of economic progress and political freedom as the most violent disruption of the placid routines of social and political life. Rome was certainly stable in the age of the Antonines. Gibbon's sonorous and wistful periods have hopelessly sentimentalized and falsified the age by stripping it of all verisimilitude and presenting it as an age of apotheosis, with its sublime but precarious equipoise of forces, and its men of rank and birth walking the earth like gods, olympian in bearing and conduct, and purged of all the unregenerate impulses and emotions. But whatever the realities of the age of the Antonines may have been, it had not the least difficulty in maintaining the senator in his villa, the servile classes in their hovels, and lesser breeds in their appointed subordination. Stability at this culminating moment of Roman ascendancy was a servitude for millions; and a starved and straitened servitude at that, for farming methods remained as stable as society. For the men and women who had been trapped in such circumstances the Dark Ages were not a long night but a tremendous liberation.

The achievement of imperial Rome in imposing an uncompromisingly uniform structure of civil government upon the borderlands of the Mediterranean and upon much of the European interior has had no equal in western history apart from the achievement of ecclesiastical Rome in imposing a comparable uniformity upon the spiritual government of European society in the Middle Ages. If the climax of the imperial system came in the first and second centuries A.D., the climax of the ecclesiastical system came in the thirteenth century A.D. when triumphant Church Councils raised the pretensions of ecclesiasticism to their highest point and the adroit manipulation of political forces by the Pope gave him an authority in European affairs the like of which he was never to enjoy again.

The recalcitrance of European spiritual life, however—its bitter, implacable defiance of the symmetry and stability proclaimed and enforced by the Church of Rome—is some measure of the limitations and the presumption of this post-classical Roman dominion. The Albigensian Crusade and the Inquisition demonstrated that there were no depths the Church would not plumb, and no expense of spirit it would not incur, in its own defence. And yet at the heart of this monolithic church was a capriciousness which the menace of the Inquisition twisted into a sinister incalculability. Perhaps there is no better epitome of this arbitrary and unpredictable quality than the story of the first audience granted by Innocent III to Francis of Assisi. At this audience Cardinal John of St Paul had to remind the Pope that when he objected to the purposes that Francis sought his permission to pursue, on the ground that striving to live according to the Gospel meant striving to do something that was beyond the strength of man, he was committing the blasphemy of declaring that Christ had conjured men to do what was impossible.[8] For one tremendous moment the balance trembled between canonization and martyrdom. For Francis the balance tilted one way; but for how many unwitting heresiarchs was it to tilt the other? Autocracy, ordained and developed in the name of stability, having bred a labyrinthine wilfulness, was in fact converting stability into its opposite.

In the end stability in religion turned out to be neither stable nor religious; and ecclesiastical Rome presently described the same trajectory of decline and fall as imperial Rome had done before. There were the same internal convulsions; the same scandals and insurrections; there was the same harsh retrenchment, followed by dismemberment; the survival of an ecclesiastical rump very like the Byzantine rump that survived the fall of Rome; and the same sense of liberation from a nightmare of tyranny and obscurantism in Europe, once strenuous Protestantism had exhausted itself and the Christian furnace had dwindled to a soft after-glow.

Politicians and historians may concur in deprecating anything that disturbs social equilibrium, and economists, gathering a formidable but unholy alliance of interests and pressure groups to their support, may set the seal of their approval upon economic policies which put stability high on their list of desirable objectives.

[8] J. R. Moorman, *An History of the Franciscan Order*, Oxford University Press, 1968, pp. 18–19.

But stability does not suit the human temperament; or perhaps it would be nearer the truth to say that stability suits the human temperament all too well. The conquering imperial power, the comfortably established ruling class, and the well-situated monopolist, ask for nothing better than a quiet life. It is mere ingenuousness to suppose that epochs which combined instability with progress, and businesses which seem to have thriven despite uncertainty, would have done even better in more stable conditions. And the attempt to achieve such conditions, by turning an economic problem into a political one, has often done more harm than the instability it was intended to mitigate. Countries which supply the world's demands for food and raw materials, for example, have been more grievously damaged by stabilization schemes than ever they were by free trade, despite the notorious volatility of world prices. Price fluctuations can always be moderated by dealings in futures; and it has always been open to growers and merchants alike to meet the losses incurred in bad years out of the savings made from the profits of good ones. But there is no futures market to protect growers from government mishandling and caprice; and whilst harassed and driven politicians promulgate contradictory policies in the name of compromise, confuse their objectives, change their minds, embezzle funds, or convert them fraudulently to other public uses than the ones for which they were intended, and consequently bewilder and bemuse all who have to attend to their pronouncements, it is likely that everyone would be better off if only they would leave the growers alone.[9]

But stability is only one of the appealing policies which his consciousness of a statesmanlike responsibility towards the community, and his agreeable sense of the popularity of grandiose projects, may tempt a politician to pursue. They are easily persuaded that if building up an industry will yield falling unit costs because of economies of scale then the thing must be done despite the fact that perfectly capable businessmen have obviously decided that the potential market did not warrant the risk. The businessmen may be wrong. But even if they are, how can the politicians and their advisers tell? Their ancestors slew animals and dabbled in their

[9] Professor P. T. Bauer has written voluminously upon this topic. See also A. I. MacBean, *Export Instability and Economic Development*, Allen & Unwin, 1966.

G

entrails. They manipulate equations. Is the change an improvement? Since 1945 Europe has been a laboratory of experiments in economic affairs. An observer of these experiments will surely be acquitted of partisanship if he concludes from them that the most remarkable economic developments have occurred in countries where central planning is least important; that the most disastrous mistakes have been made in the most planned of all economic activities, which is farming; and that the worst mistakes in planning farming have been made where such planning has been comprehensive and inquisitorial, as in Russia, and the least harmful ones where the reins were loosest, as in Denmark and Poland. Change has been so rapid since 1945 that the European economic scene is littered with the debris of bankrupt enterprises and unfulfilled hopes. But where central planners have been at work the debris dominates the view : coal-mines lavishly appointed for an age of oil and nuclear power; steel industries equipped for an age of plastics; railways modernized for an age of cars and aeroplanes.[10]

Even did the statesmanlike view make politicians adept at picking the right economic activities to promote, they would still be left with crucial problems which obstinately defy solution. By what obscure sibylline communings with occult powers, by what anxious appeal to their econometric advisers, are they to be equipped to decide how much to invest in their chosen enterprises?

The problem is eased by business depression, when resources are idle. Money spent by governments in such circumstances need not deprive consumers of what they might otherwise have been able to buy, or investors of opportunities which they might otherwise have been able to take. But deep and widespread depression was unusual before the twentieth century. The more familiar problem was one of underemployment of labour due to famine scarcities of capital. In such conditions plans to occupy idle hands that the Devil always found work for were legion, and invariably attract the favourable notice of historians concerned with prob-

[10] On grounds of public welfare there is an overwhelming case for putting aeroplanes and cars in their place instead of allowing them to reduce our cities to noisome squalor. But railways were not modernized with this in mind. They were modernized for a traditional role by planners who got their forecasts wrong.

lems of poor relief. But they generally involved the diversion of capital from existing uses and therefore proposed changes which were more likely to alter the structure of employment than its volume. This means that, for practical purposes, politicians with flamboyant schemes to promote have usually had to plan on the assumption that their investments would reduce present consumption for the sake of the future.

Depriving the present for the sake of the future hands some of the wealth of the present forward in time. Future generations cannot be better off than present ones if some wealth is not handed on in this way. But the problem is : how much? as well as : in what form? 'From some points of view,' remarked D. H. Robertson : [11]

> the whole cycle of industrial change presents the appearance
> of a perpetual immolation of the present upon the altar of
> the future. During the boom sacrifices are made out of all
> proportion to the enjoyment over which they will ultimately
> give command; during the depression enjoyment is denied
> lest it should debar the possibility of making fresh sacrifices.
> Out of the welter of industrial dislocation the great permanent
> riches of the future are generated. How far are we bound to
> honour the undrawn bills of posterity, and to acquiesce in this
> never-closing hyperbola of intersecular exchange?

The sacrifices might be more intelligible if the risks were not so great; and the risks multiply as the time-scale lengthens into the future. The risks are greatest in the poorest countries where the margin of safety is, by definition, slenderest; and where, indeed, the question of sacrificing anything at all in order to take a chance on contributing something towards the enrichment of posterity is one to which there is no self-evident answer. But even when the risks are slighter, and the time-scale dwindles from decades to years, or even to months, an essential problem remains. Embarking upon new investments means shifting resources from existing employment to new ones. It means depriving consumers of one set of services and products and hoping that with improvements and, perhaps, lower prices, they will be compensated for their loss by the new pattern of services and products that the

[11] D. H. Robertson, *A Study of Industrial Fluctuation*, L.S.E. Reprints of Scarce Works on Political Economy, no. 8, 1948, p. 254.

investments will yield to them. But time travels in one direction only; the losses are irretrievable; when the changes have been made the consumers and their circumstances will be changed too. How does one quantify the losses, measure the compensation afforded by the changes, and allow for the passage of time?

In a competitive world where the consumer votes by buying or refraining from buying, and time-discounts can be expressed in terms of rates of interest, one may hope that voting will bring about some sort of rough justice. But in a planner's world, the risks and the losses, the sacrifices and the distortions, are cheerfully dismissed by politicians who plan and build, restrict and license, tax and subsidize, in the name of modernization, economic growth, defence, social justice, full employment and the like. The frenzy of nationalism, which they themselves have usually done much to incite, takes possession of them and infects their policies with a fatal lavishness. Late development ceases to mean learning from the mistakes of others. Instead it means making a new kind of mistake: the mistake of buying the latest, most elaborate, and technically most complex equipment, from the most advanced countries in the world, regardless of the needs of the community, which may have emerged only recently from primitive conditions, and apparently with every mark of enthusiastic approval by the historians.

When Russian engineers went abroad, in the late nineteenth century, to buy equipment for their iron and steel industry, they bought German equipment as soon as German technology had outstripped British, and American as soon as American technology had outstripped German. Meanwhile, at home, careless and ignorant railwaymen floundered and blundered their way to some sort of understanding of the management of rolling-stock and permanent way at immense cost to the system that the state had thrust into their keeping. Professor Gerschenkron has defended this policy of buying the most sophisticated equipment available on the ground that where skills are as scarce as they were in nineteenth-century Russia, substituting machinery for skill will release skill for other employment, and justified the policy by pointing to the spectacular rate of increase of output achieved.[12]

But skill, in this sense, was not the only resource that was

[12] A. Gerschenkron, *Economic Backwardness in Historical Perspective*, Harvard University Press, 1962, chapter 6, *passim*.

scarce in nineteenth-century Russia. It was not even the one that was most scarce. Capital in all its multitudinous forms was that. Only if capital had been as abundant in nineteenth-century Russia as skill was scarce would there have been anything to be said for the insensate prodigality of Russian spending. And only if the Russian iron and steel industry had not been sheltered from foreign competition by an insurmountable tariff, and had not been presented with a market for railway and military material which the government sustained and expanded with every scrap of financial ingenuity at its command, would there have been any significance in the output figures. As it was, the Russian consumer was bled white, the Russian industrialist was surfeited, the Russian state gathered to itself more power than it had ever enjoyed before, and there emerged from all the bustle, and waste, and confusion, a renovated Juggernaut, or rather an ungainly medieval Russian knight, clanking his modern steel armour, and fingering a little uncertainly the unfamiliar weapons of the nineteenth century, as he postured truculently before his imperialist neighbours. The world, however, took this Russian mountebank very seriously; and the historian is nothing if he is not a man of the world.

In countries where there was more scope for private initiative, and the temptation to indulge in ostenstatious spending was curbed by humdrum considerations of profitability, the story was very different. When German businessmen went abroad for textile machinery, in the late nineteenth century, they were well content to buy second-hand. And they bought second-hand, not because their workers were so very much more expert than Russian workers that they could make do with second-best, but because they were acutely conscious that their workers were not good enough for anything else.[13] What struck German businessmen about Lancashire in the 1880s was the character of the Lancashire worker, who was so very different from their own. He was punctual, reliable, skilful, resourceful, conscientious, and fully habituated to the rhythm and discipline of industrial life. Complex machines and simple workmen, with a few instructions in their heads and the uncomplicated routines of farmyard and domestic system in their bones, did not mix then, and did not mix later, as the

[13] G. von Schulze-Gaevernitz, *The Cloth Trade in England and on the Continent*, Simpkin Marshall, 1895.

Tanganyika groundnuts scheme taught the British taxpayer in 1948.[14]

But historians, as a class, do not take to piecemeal development, and are not afflicted by scruples as to the economic and political implications of vast accomplishments. They want heroes and economic miracles; they adore the unparalleled and the unprecedented. They tell the story of German textiles because it is there to be told. What enthralls and intoxicates them, however, is the technological virtuosity and phenomenal growth of the German electrical, chemical, and steel industries. Nothing can detract from the German record of industrial advance, which is surpassed, perhaps, only by that of Japan. An industrious people, highly educated at the technical and professional levels, highly skilled as craftsmen, their country rich in bituminous coal and potash salts, with ready access to excellent supplies of iron ore, the Germans had much to favour their rapid development. But their political masters dreamt dreams of astounding the world with the power of Germany rather than with the wealth and prosperity of its citizens. Making Germany powerful meant keeping ordinary Germans poorer than they might otherwise have been, and less free. But theirs was not the choice. Momentous things were done in Germany in the name of defence, prestige, and rational planning, which incomparably strengthened the hands of the government and of its chief financial and industrial coadjutors, and held back the rise of the real income of the ordinary German consumer. Between them, the state which gave unstinted aid to what it took to be indispensably important industries, and the industrial banks, which dominated the supply of investment funds, foreclosed competition, took crucial decisions as to the size and structure of certain key industries, and then, in effect, gave the development engineers their head. It was, in a sense, a foreshadowing of the American space programme. The results, in both cases, were spectacular. The incidental benefits derived by more prosaic activities from discoveries and improvements made in the pursuit of solutions to other problems, were important. But what of the costs?

When markets are competitive the question of costs does not

[14] This was not the only lesson that the groundnuts scheme taught the taxpayer. Nor was it the most important one. See Alan Wood, *The Groundnuts Affair*, Bodley Head, 1950.

arise. Firms either pay their way or go bankrupt. Inefficient firms do survive because factors of production are not perfectly mobile between uses, and because some industrial costs are met by the taxpayer, who provides facilities for all which in fact subsidize industrial users, and by the private citizen, who must endure the vexatious and noisome consequences of industrial activities, usually without any compensation whatsoever. Inefficient firms get no more than their share of these uncovenanted benefits; but since these benefits keep down the costs that must be met if a firm is to survive they help to explain the level of inefficiency that any particular competitive economy will tolerate. These reservations apart, however, and taking the vigilance of the government and the distribution of income for granted, the competitive system will see to it that costs are more or less what they should be.

These are important reservations and large assumptions; and everyone knows that the practice of competition is very different from the theory. It would be a grotesque misrepresentation, for example, to call the American oil and railway businesses competitive in the days of Rockefeller and Vanderbilt. Nevertheless a deep gulf separates a competitive system which often works badly and sometimes breaks down altogether from a system which moved the Austrian Consul in Berlin to report in 1906 that German industrial life was ruled by barely fifty men who between them decided output, exports, prices, wages, rates of interest, the granting of credit, and the raising of capital. No doubt he exaggerated. But when movement between economic activities was as closely controlled as it was in Germany before 1914, and historians invite the world to share their admiration of the results, then the question of costs is very much in order.

Historians see the ominous concentration of power; they see the bankers concerting their plans untrammelled by the constraints of competition or public accountability; they see the subsidies and the rebates, the tariffs and the concessions. But the technological proficiency of German industry, and the output figures which they set out with such ingenuous pleasure and unqualified admiration, blind them to the persistent backwardness and penury of much of German life; to the inherent dangers and well-known shortcomings of any system which subdues competition to a conspiracy and settles vital questions of resource allocation behind closed doors instead of in the market place; and to the disquieting implications of these developments for the liberty of the subject in Germany.

They applaud the brilliance of German research and development. But they entirely ignore the immense costs incurred by any programme of successful innovation. A mature industrial economy with comparatively abundant resources can take in its stride the ideas that prove to be barren, the experiments that go wrong, the products that pass every laboratory test but run into intractable manufacturing difficulties, and the items in every salesman's catalogue that do everything that can possibly be expected of them, except sell. But a country new to industrialization cannot spare resources for such hazards. Its urgent needs are for the individually simple things that taken together make up the familiar setting of an industrialized society: bridges and tunnels; docks and harbours; civic utilities and amenities; houses by the million, factories by the score. The list is endless, but not glamorous. A rural society making the transition to full industrialization will neglect it, however, at its peril. The Japanese made themselves ridiculous in western eyes, between the wars, by imitating the industrial processes and products of advanced countries instead of striking out with innovations of their own. The imitations were often slavish and sometimes, when the originals were defective, reproduced these defects to the vast amusement of those who watched uncomprehendingly from afar. But copying with discrimination means profiting by the experience of others. It is the providence of the underdeveloped economy. Historians who prefer the German example to the Japanese, where they differ, need a better justification for their preference than the resounding performance of the major German industries.

Behind advanced technology lies education; and historians who are themselves, usually, distinguished members of the teaching profession, esteem the Germans for their generous endowment of education and their idolatrous respect for research. But the German system produced a glut: young men of intelligence and ambition for whom there was no professional future except abroad. Education has always been an important asset to ambitious young men with nothing but their wits about them. It has made them socially mobile. When prospects at home were poor, as they often were in Scotland, it gave them the edge over other migrants seeking fame and fortune abroad. Sometimes it carried them against the tide of migration, as it did in the early twentieth century when Britain, which had colonized an empire with her sons, began to repatriate her brighter and better educated grandsons from Australia and New Zealand, from Canada and South Africa, to staff her professions with. But the German migration of clerks and artisans, engineers and scientists, was on an altogether different scale : it was a mass exodus fed by the system of commercial and technical education that attracted much respectful admiration from English contemporaries and now provides historians who are critical of Britain's industrial performance with a stick with which to beat anyone who can be held responsible for the comparative neglect of public education in England from the mid-nineteenth century onwards.

Migration is obviously beneficial to a congested country, particularly if it lowers the political temperatures as it relieves the congestion. Unfortunately migration, by calling to those with energy, youth, and a sense of adventure, calls to those whom no country can really afford to lose. When it also calls to the trained and educated classes, then loss begins to outweigh gain with a vengeance. Germany's losses, by this reckoning, were immense. They must be set with the other costs of national aggrandizement and militarization that historians so often agree to ignore.

6   Big business

From certain points of view business is the state in microcosm; and the economic historian passes easily therefore from ardent and reverential admiration of the one to rapturous enthusiasm for the other. His political judgment may endorse a famous interpretation of the Sherman Act which saw it as an honourable attempt, made in the name of the liberty of the subject, 'to perpetuate and preserve for its own sake, and in spite of possible cost, an organization of industry in small units which can effectively compete with each other.'[1] His knowledge of the way of the world, powerfully reinforced by Professor Parkinson's devastating portrayal of the self-perpetuating and self-fructifying dangers of bureaucracy, should set him inflexibly against any form of centralized and monopolistic enterprise for which there is not an overwhelming and unanswerable case on grounds of altogether exceptional circumstances and needs. And his training in economic theory ought to remind him that until very recently economies of scale meant, for most businesses, a size which left plenty of room for vigorous competition, and that even today the case for expanding all but a very few businesses beyond that size, in the interests of such economics, is strenuously contested on theoretical grounds.

But considerations such as these are not proof against the intoxication that overwhelms the historian who identifies himself with the great captains of industry and with the immense organizations that express their insatiable will to dominate. And he is a rare creature indeed who can make such men and such organizations his professional concern without succumbing to the glamour of their personalities and achievements. For big business exercises a perennial and, for the most part, an irresistible fascination upon historians. Biographies of the great men of business,

[1] Cited in Walter Adams (ed), *The Structure of American Industry*, Macmillan, New York, third edition, 1965, p. 533.

ancient and modern, read more like hagiography than anything else. And accounts of the organizations these men created manage to combine the rotund complacencies of the company report with the brash salesmanship of the company prospectus.

The great man of business etches upon ivory where the great political leader plasters huge canvasses with his garish colours. He cannot redraw maps, dictate frontiers, supplant dynasties, promulgate ordinances, codify laws. He cannot fling armies across the world at recalcitrant adversaries, or crush sedition in blood. But the story of rags to riches has the same compelling quality as the more traditional story of humble cabin to imperial palace. As told by the professional historian it dispenses with none of the accessory paraphernalia that go with the unfolding of the portentous melodrama of the career of a Caesar or a Napoleon : the painstaking and wearisome genealogical tables tracing the wonderful man back to his remotest known forebears; the wooden portraits of bleary sires and grimly puritanical dams; the extracts from letters and papers in which our hero moralizes nauseatingly, in his flat and sententious prose, on the morrow of success; the tedious catalogue of subsequent triumphs over rivals; the citations from adulatory contemporaries used as evidence of qualities beyond the ordinary; the sketches and photographs of residencies; the diligent computation of riches.

Like other empire-builders, the successful man of business defies classification. He is not always a shameless buccaneer. He may be shy, and lonely, and sensitive to the point of psychological unbalance. He may be a miser or a philanthropist; a toiler or a trifler; a man of honour or a poltroon; a chuckle-headed gambler of genius or a shrewd and assiduous man of affairs ruthlessly subordinating every consideration to an unfalteringly accurate calculation of the main chance. Like other men, though perhaps in greater degree, he may be something of all these things. But he is unlikely to have invented anything or discovered anything, though he is uncannily quick to perceive the practical value of other men's ideas, and readily brings the dedication of a saint to purposes which range from the frivolous to the downright criminal. But his essential talents lie elsewhere. He can organize; and he can sell. Best of all he can sell himself : for one of his greatest assets is his power to inspire confidence in men with money to lend, or advantages to confer.

Thus equipped, and driven by an overmastering urge to make his mark in the world, the successful man of business embarks upon a career of self-advancement as inexorably aggressive as any that sweeps other men to political power and imperial conquest, and less damaging to society only because there are weapons he may not use. He rarely starts from a position of overwhelming advantage over other men. There may be a propitious marriage, a bountiful patron, or influential contacts, to hasten his progress. He may even inherit a business already showing promise of great things. But, generally speaking, he enters the world of business as one competitor amongst many, even though he will leave it as a monopolist.

Becoming a monopolist is, indeed, the crown and climax of his career; for monopoly in one or other of its myriad forms is the goal towards which competitive business hurries with all the speed it may. Fighting may be instinctive to man; but fighting without hope of victory, fighting, in fact, for the sheer love of it, must quickly tire even the most aggressive spirit. And victory in business, as in war, means conquest or terms. At one extreme, it means the annihilation of rivals and the expropriation of their resources; at the other, it means truce, a pause between bouts, a respite from mutual spoliation. Between these extremes there is room for every kind of accommodation : for competition restricted to relatively few participants who may further agree, as in the professions, to constrain their rivalry within clearly defined boundaries; for competition limited by area or product; for competition confined to quality or ancillary services. The ingenuity of such devices is inexhaustible; and the permutations and combinations to which they give rise must run into millions.

In theory the competition that businessmen are so anxious to foreclose can be endlessly renewed by the entry of new firms into industry. The prizes of victory then dwindle into the modest returns necessary to prevent resources from being attracted into other occupations; historians have no heroes to glorify; and businessmen struggle and contend simply in order to make a living, not because they have had the misfortune to be caught in a declining or a depressed trade, but because they have had the misfortune to be caught in a competitive one.

The world we know, however, cannot meet the stringent requirements of theory. At best the transfer of resources from one occupation to another takes time and trouble. Knowledge is invariably meagre or inadequate; mobility is always hampered by men who cling to their skills even more tenaciously than to their homes, and by the longevity of buildings and machines which cannot be successfully adapted to new uses. Habit dominates those who buy as well as those who sell, even when it is not conditioned and strengthened by advertising and other forms of promotion. And patents, restrictive covenants, collusive arrangements between groups of businessmen or working men, and government intervention on behalf of powerful factions which stand to lose by change, all conspire to take the resilience out of economic life in an attempt to protect the status and safeguard the prosperity of sectional interests.

The world of business may be a jungle; and the law of the jungle may be harsh. But its harsh law does not make the business jungle competitive except in the loose sense that it is a struggle for survival. Competition as a means of allocating resources efficiently is not something that occurs naturally in the absence of restraint. It depends very largely upon the success with which the community can oppose and minimize the political power of coalitions of businessmen and associations of working men. It depends, in short, upon the favourable outcome of the perennial problem of reconciling the strenuous trumpet-tongued importunities of faction with the freedom and independence of the individual. It is therefore as contrived and yet as precious as anything that can be achieved by political action in the name of liberty. Its real enemy is not capitalism, or socialism, or any other fashionable nostrum, or rallying cry of the streets. Its real enemy is monopoly in all its forms. Salvation lies, therefore, in keeping the politically powerful divided, and if possible peaceably at enmity with one another, and in making sure that the government itself accumulates no more real authority than it needs in order to be able to cope with likely combinations of interests. And it lies in private business, subdued by rivalry instead of fostered and nourished by government patronage, and disciplined either by the daily verdict of the market-place, or where necessary, by the inviolable rulings of a monopolies commission.

Such a system requires unremitting vigilance; and since vigilance implies knowledge, it requires the full disclosure of matters at present rendered inaccessible by such hallowed defences of incompetence, scandal, and clandestine manipulation, as the law of libel, the Official Secrets Act, and the virtual impotence of existing institutional means of investigating matters of legitimate public concern that enables public servants, professional men, and leading notables in all spheres of life, to express with impunity their dignified and authoritative repudiation of responsibility for doing or failing to do things that everyone knows they should or should not have done.

Everything militates against the enforcement of competition conceived of in these terms. Business rejects it for all its protestations of faith in freedom; trade unions fear it; the professions fight it bitterly, upon the slightest provocation, with every weapon in their armoury; and national pride can be cleverly worked upon or indeed spontaneously outraged, by competitive threats to the future of great businesses which seem to symbolize national prestige or national achievement, or by the failure of the government to support the establishment of businesses for which there is no possible justification except for the satisfaction they give to those who fulfil themselves by the quaint indulgence of paying the taxes that keep them going.

It is in the context of vital issues such as these that historians throw the weight of their authority against the forces making for freedom, and hence for equality before the law, in politics, and even, perhaps, in social life. As citizens of communities in which liberty ranks high, if not first, amongst cherished political ideals, they know very well that liberty calls for indefatigable resistance to enchroachments disguised as emancipation; to repression got up to look like maintenance of law and order; and to discrimination against persons somehow miraculously purged of humbug by blasphemous appeals to religion, by the sanctimonious invocation of tradition, or by the simple but sublime consciousness of the moral superiority of the white races, or the aristocratic and professional classes, or western technological man, over the common run of mortals. As historians, however, they allow their judgments to be hopelessly perverted by the values of the business jungle. Their heroes are the seigneur not the serf; the employer not the wage-earner; the producer not the consumer; the flourishing trade union, itself a triumph of orthodox commercial principles, not the working classes. A good harvest is a harvest which raises profits, not a harvest which increases consumption.

A successful businessman is one who has made a fortune out of his enterprises, not necessarily one who has treated his workers decently, or kept his prices as low as he could instead of conspiring with others to keep them as high as possible. A thriving economy is one where equipment is modern and fixed, and capital is kept at full stretch, not one where living standards are the first consideration, where income distribution is equitable, and where relationships between men at work are civilized.

History is bound to be steeped in monopoly because the past is full of it. If the great captains of commerce and industry created monopolies they did so in a world of monopoly. They seized the opportunities that came their way and exploited them to the full just as the great military and political leaders exploited the opportunities of their times to carve immortal reputations out of war and diplomacy. But historians whose highest political aspiration is to see freedom flourish according to the liberal canons to which they subscribe, are not required by the exigencies of their profession to grovel in adulation before the monopolies they have to investigate and portray, as some do, or to succumb to the fascination of the masterful personalities and overwhelming power of those who presided over the stertorous behemoths that so often dominated some vital sphere of economic activity.

When coal made industrial Europe grimy, the grime made the fortunes of the men in soap. Of these men William Lever was king. Lever may have left the soap industry very much as he found it : a congeries of small and medium-sized firms using traditional methods of production and making few attempts to improve the washing qualities of their soaps. But he perceived for the first time that soap wrapped in decorative paper would make an irresistible appeal to housewives accustomed to ordering a cut off the communal bar from the grocer who also sliced her bacon from a communal side. To the flair of a salesman of genius, Lever added the gifts, as well as the looks, of the circus ring-master, and swept an impressionable generation off its feet with his advertising. The result was transcendent success which brought retribution in its wake only when acquisitiveness got the better of him and his ramshackle empire threatened to collapse under its own weight. D'Arcy Cooper then rescued Lever Brothers very much as Alfred Sloan rescued General Motors, which William Durant had driven to a similar pass.

Lever's business life was probably unexceptionable; he was a bold, energetic, and imaginative figure; and he controlled an impressive aggregation of resources. Who could bear to see so dazzling a career end in disaster, or so commanding an empire dissolve? Everyone who reads the official history is invited to breathe a sigh of relief once health is restored to the Lever empire and Lever himself dies full of honours and years.

And yet what was it that D'Arcy Cooper rescued? The appeal of a career such as Lever's obscures the dangerous problem set by the growth of huge corporations in a competitive economy and in a society struggling towards political freedom. Even when some buccaneering career has so far trespassed beyond the generous limits of permissible public misdemeanour that the worshipping backs straighten in momentary dismay and homage gives place to obloquy, matters are only improved to the extent that revulsion from the captain of industry and all his works is possibly a healthier emotion than hero-worship. But the essential point is missed as much by those who are sharply critical as by those who are fulsome in their approbation.

What matters about Lever, and other men like him, is not their personal conduct or their public careers. These things are of no account compared with the social and political consequences of their achievements. Rockefeller is an infinitely more controversial figure than Lever. But what matters about Rockefeller is not whether he schemed and plotted like some incarnation of duplicity, or played the game like a gentleman. What matters is that he took a fairly competitive oil industry and turned it into a monopoly which in the closing years of the nineteenth century refined and distributed over eighty per cent of all the oil produced in America. In doing so he imposed a trim pattern of organization upon a profusion of competing firms, and built enormous refineries of great technical complexity. For this he gets full marks; as he does for the charitable uses to which he devoted profits whose staggering magnitude ought to have disconcerted even his most infatuated partisan.

Yet it is the thing that is praised that is most deplorable. The monopoly created by Rockefeller was intolerable on social and political grounds and indefensible on economic grounds. The immense size and integrated structure of the oil company have become familiar features of modern life. Historians mistaking what is for what must be hail Rockefeller as the architect and pioneer of necessary innovations and developments. But historians who are ready enough, in mercantilist mood, to see measures which were conducive to economic progress compelled to defer to the needs of autarky, which set national glory high above individual well-being, are in no position to cavil at the suggestion that necessary innovations and developments in business, when these innovations and developments threaten society with monopoly, could equally well be compelled to defer to the more desirable objective of safe-guarding the competitive health of the economy.

Not that Rockefeller's innovations and developments were necessary ones. Recent work upon the economics of the oil industry indicates that the world's major oil companies are not so much businesses as political powers, and that, even today, when technology has become very much more sophisticated than it was in Rockefeller's day, their size and structure have much less to do with the requirements of finance and technology than with their version of what is known in other circles as the armaments race.[2]

It is of this race that Rockefeller was the pioneer. The tremendous structure of integrated businesses and fixed plant that became Standard Oil, far from being a necessary condition of efficient functioning in the late nineteenth century, was in fact nothing but the cover for a gigantic stabilization scheme of which the bene-ficiaries were not the government, as it so often is when primary-producing countries resort to such schemes, but Rockefeller and his associates. The story of American oil has many affinities with that of other primary products, even to the pretexts for stabiliza-tion, which it shares with them. It began with fantastic profits which gave producers and refiners an exaggerated notion of normal profits and made them discontented when those profits disappeared. The fluctuations were wild; but the profits matched them; and well-conducted businesses, which did not mistake high profits for normal ones, and made sensible provision for lean years, won through. The situation, however, was ripe for stabilization; and Rockefeller's achievement was to bring it about. What America paid for his work is probably beyond computation. He imposed upon a vital industry a structure it did not require and

[2] Edith T. Penrose, *The Large International Firm in Developing Countries*, Allen & Unwin, 1968.

H

never subsequently shook off, and a level of technological proficiency which deprived other sectors of a rapidly growing
economy of resources and skills which they could probably have
put to far more productive use. The stupendous profits of
Standard Oil are some measure of the ransom he extorted. But
his true memorial is perhaps the progressive deterioration of the
quality of American life, for which the second American Civil
War, the one that he and his fellow tycoons waged in order to
establish private empires in the American economy, must take its
large share of blame.

Historians of business are not, however, greatly troubled by
such considerations. For them, as for Sarah Battle, the game is
the thing. As a rule, therefore, biographies of the outstanding
leaders of business are as oblivious of the dangerous consequences
of the concentration of economic power as studies of outstanding
national leaders are of the cost in life, liberty, and the pursuit
of happiness, of the terrible paths their heroes so carelessly trod.[3]

In this respect economic history is perhaps the last refuge of
Victorian optimism. The central theme of economic history is
improvement, frequently interrupted, sometimes reversed, but
gathering pace over the centuries, as wealth accumulated and
standards of living rose, and culminating in the unparalleled
transformation of society which is the dominant feature of modern
times. Monopolistic enterprises, although protected by law and
private treaty from presumptuous interlopers, have nevertheless
acquired a colouring of respectability from their association with
this material progress. It is hard to believe that big business, which
has about it so convincing an air of success, did not make an
indispensable contribution to the story. Consequently historians
never tire of regaling their readers with biographies of merchants
and manufacturers, ancient and modern, who having done well
and married better, then acquired the ear of an influential patron,
and, by toadying to him, accumulated the means with which to
raise their posterity to a position not much inferior, if at all, to
that of their benefactor.

Industrialization may have modified the details of this trumpery progression to the extent that the patron is no longer to be
found at court, but in the government, or in the government

[3] Even the robber barons now get their meed of praise: see Peter d'A.
Jones, *The Robber Barons Revisited*, Heath, Boston, 1968.

department, or at party headquarters. But the benefactions continue to protect and to privilege in recognizable ways; and the sentiments expressed by those who give and those who take, the unctuous professions of concern for the welfare of the community, the declarations of selfless devotion to the highest ideals of service, differ only in cadence and phrasing from those uttered by earlier generations of patrons and beneficiaries.

And the story is as banal as its political morals are scandalous. Pitch six spirited young men into the middle of the Pacific Ocean on a tiny raft with little more to do than keep alive and watch the sea and the sky, and they presently discover for themselves that there is more to the sea than water and more to the sky than air. 'We lived . . . with alert intensity. We realized that life had been full for men before the technical age also—indeed fuller and richer in many ways than the life of modern man.'[4] Pitch six historians into the ocean of business history, and unless they have the gifts that enable some writers to turn the most unpromising material into dramatic poetry, they will discover nothing more instructive or edifying about past leaders of the business world than the external facts of successful careers, and the commonplaces of otherwise ordinary lives, with their desultory irregularities and idiosyncrasies. For the secret of achievement in business, as in other spheres of human endeavour, they will look in vain. It is locked for ever from the gaze of bystanders. The trick is done; the world is all breathless admiration; but the conjurer cannot tell the secret of his skill even if he would. When he dies his secret dies with him; what remains, if anything does, is such tangible evidence of accomplishment as there may be, and memories, and gossip.

Historians who are disposed to take a more profane view of the contribution of monopolistic business to economic development may nevertheless be tempted to comfort themselves with the reflection that the power of monopoly has waned. The worst days of monopoly were those when usurer and bailiff filled the village sky with a dread greater than any that the Church could inspire with threats of damnation. Their extortions were more or less inescapable because travel was difficult, opportunities elsewhere were few, and the wanderers ran imminent risk of seizure as a

[4] Thor Heyerdahl, *The Kon-Tiki Expedition*, Allen & Unwin, 1950, p. 132.

vagrant, or worse. As travel improved, and opportunities multiplied, local monopoly lost its virulence and competition destroyed
its power. The competition may have been the competition of
industries which would presently supplant lesser monopolies by
a greater. But with the widening of markets went a diversification
of industry which gave the consumer a choice of things to buy,
and the wage-earner a choice of occupation and employment.
The changes came slowly; fortuitous interruptions and interruptions which were not fortuitous may have retarded the rate of
change; but in a longer perspective successive monopolies have
been deprived of their power on the morrow of achieving it.

This is a reassuring doctrine which fails, however, to allow
for the gathering power and influence of the forces of modern
monopoly. Consumers have always benefited by competition
even when they have been so conditioned as not to welcome it;
business has always been anxious to dispense with it. Consumers are
many; businesses are comparatively few. Restraining competition
can always be made to appear to be able to do more good to the
individual business, therefore, than it does harm to the individual
consumer. Moreover business is organized and consumers are
not. In the struggle between them business has always had the
advantage, and consequently the historian's favour. And if
government has ever been at pains to curb its excesses or silence
its importunities, business has met every check with a dozen
subterfuges. In such encounters no government can hope to fore-
stall business, because effective policy can only be formulated
after the event. Hence business interests, when they cannot expect
to be able to rely upon government because it is their creature or
their devoted patron, can generally count upon long delays before
their latest restrictive practices are forbidden, and even longer
ones before they are stopped, or at any rate checked.

Sometimes the delay is inordinate because business, acting with
consummate guile, raises the cry of freedom in defence of its
practices, to the consternation of those who genuinely cherish
freedom and fear any threat to it. Modern technology has created
an industry out of the art of imposing the will of the businessman
upon the whim of the consumer by every means short of intimidation and the use of physical violence. And this industry now has
the distinction of having prodigiously widened the market for
many products and enormously increased the size and power of

certain firms, without having run into the serious trouble it so richly deserves. For skilful promotion, by its calculated rascality, has done untold harm. In many industries it has destroyed competition and put in its place the circumspect antagonisms of rival giants. It has disfigured the streets and even the countryside. It dominates the newspapers. It strengthens rich industries at the expense of poorer ones and thus, in the end, deprives the consumer of things he once could have had, because what is not cried up stands only a slim chance of surviving at all. It lies strenuously and more or less with impunity, and distorts and misrepresents when it does not actually lie, without running serious risk of prosecution for false description.

The cost of doing all this is heavy, partly because consumers have to be won over from spending their money on other things, and partly because they have to be induced to buy from one firm rather than from its competitors. Wider markets have enabled businesses to take advantage of economies of scale which were beyond their reach when they were smaller and which inspire the facile claim that promotion reduces costs. The individual firm may indeed produce more cheaply than it could have done without promoting its wares; though it may be, as the case of the Lever soap empire shows, that successful promotion wins the firm a preeminence so unassailable that it does not bother greatly about costs. And even when it does, the task of comparing its costs before it started to promote its products with what they were later when it did, is a treacherously difficult one to carry out because promotion, when it succeeds, can easily change both firm and products out of all recognition. But the community pays a heavy price for all this highly professional huckstering, quite apart from the damage it sustains, which the hucksters are not required to make good; and the individual consumer pays too. For what is this huge investment in persuasion, at bottom, but a tremendous effort dedicated to the conviction that if only the consumer can be prevailed upon to give up what he patently prefers, because he has to be wheedled and mesmerized into forsaking it, his reward will be to get something that is, by definition, second-best, either at a price lower than it might have been if he had not been won over, or perhaps, merely in a more attractive form?

The consumer, being a reasonably sybaritic fellow, might very well feel that the game was worth the candle, and submit himself to the colourful huckstering with pleasure, or at least with a good grace, but for the arguments with which big business defends itself against the charges of those who seek to curb its spending upon the promotion of its wares. How often does big business declare that without incessant promotion there cannot be an assured mass-market for mass-produced goods, and that without an assured mass-market there must be the constant risk of losses, failure, idle resources, and unemployment! Is the implication not plain? Is it not that the consumer, unless he is constantly harassed, will presently forget how much he needed those cheap but attractive and apparently indispensable wares which mass-production alone was able to supply him with? Or is there, perhaps, another implication? Does the argument really imply that money which is not spent on the massively-promoted products of big business will not be spent at all?

In this case the wholly tendentious appeal is to the dread of the dark menace of a past when unemployment was pervasive and seemingly incurable. Slumps undoubtedly occur because money is not spent. But it is not the money of the overwhelming mass of the population that is not spent. Saving has never been a conspicuous feature of the habits of the majority of those who now make up the mass-market for mass-produced goods. Saving is done by governments, when they have a mind to it, by institutions, and by the few who have money to spare. And seeing to it that a serious decline of economic activity is offset by public spending is one of the tasks to which government is rightly committed. It is not a task which a free society can possibly permit big business to arrogate to itself.

Size is, no doubt, in itself, an impressive argument. But it is not its own justification. All too often those who are impressed by the size of certain businesses are caught up in the toils of an argument which proceeds from the impeccable observation that efficient firms sometimes grow big, to the unwarrantable conclusion that big firms are generally efficient. A big firm may very well survive determined competitive assault, despite monumental mismanagement, because sheer size and wealth keep it going. But if it is sheltered from competition by the state, or by the protean multiplicity of devices to which big firms can resort when they are not prevented from doing so, then size is no more a measure of efficiency in business than it is in government.

The only test of economic efficiency that a free society can respect is the ability to survive the unqualified competition of rivals for the unsolicited suffrage of the consumer. We have little enough experience of the operation of such a test. So far, only Britain, amongst industrial nations, has submitted itself unconditionally to the verdict of a test which is even remotely comparable with the ideal. Between 1860 and 1931, however, when Britain defied the industrially embattled might of the rest of the world virtually without benefit of tariff or subsidy, British firms remained comparatively small. It is fashionable to decry the industrial performance of Britain in that period. But if British firms did not, on the whole, gather themselves into monopolistic aggregations of commercial and industrial power, the presumption must surely be that they were more or less what competition had made them, and not necessarily the product of lethargy, improvidence, stupidity and ignorance.

The scale of things has now changed out of all recognition; and the problems set by firms which expand beyond the existing capacity of the community to discipline them, get more urgent as the rich economies grow richer. A distinguished authority on such matters has noted that the dominance of the biggest firms is now so overwhelming in America that the courts, which have an excellent record in extirpating restrictive practices and terminating cartels, find themselves at a loss in attempting to grapple with the giants, and have been reduced to expressing the full majesty of the law by lecturing them harmlessly on good behaviour.[5]

This is surely the very definition of the overmighty subject who, in earlier days, flagrantly defied the rules and set some of the most difficult problems for law and politics to solve. On the face of it, communities which are rich beyond the dreams of avarice can easily dispense with organizations which threaten their political institutions, and compromise their efforts to achieve a balance between freedom and equality, without sacrificing anything essential to their material well-being in doing so. If there is a material loss to be borne, because one or two of these giants of big business are, in fact, most efficient at the size they have achieved, then no community is better able to bear such a loss, as part of the price that it must be prepared to pay for the integrity

[5] G. C. Allen, *Monopoly and Restrictive Practices*, Allen & Unwin, 1968.

of its political institutions, than a rich one is. If there is poverty within the community, clever advocacy will contend that the contribution of big business can most expeditiously relieve it. But in so rich a community redistribution of income can readily compensate for any loss of expeditious relief, fancied or real, without causing intolerable hardship to those whose incomes are diminished.

Unfortunately wealth only changes its beneficiaries materially. The problems of politics are not less acute, therefore, in rich communities than in poor ones. And big business now commands a wider circle of admirers, particularly amongst academic writers, than it has ever done before. It has indeed taken on what is virtually a thaumaturgical sanctity: for the haunting dreams of perpetual renewal and immortal life that heartened the saints in their agonies, fortified the martyrs at the moment of immolation, inspired the poets, and redeemed metaphysics from banality, are now materializing in the shape of an immanent godhead—the modern business corporation.

Under this new dispensation, manufacture, which was once a matter of sweat-shops and domestic slavery, and later of factory work, with labour as a substantial or even a dominant cost, is now on the way to becoming a system of processes, which will banish labour from the factory except as a supervisor of flows. At the same time management is throwing off the last vestiges of control by those who own the resources it handles; and industrial enterprise, manipulating consumer taste by means of promotion, and product innovation by way of research and development, is emancipating itself from earlier dependence upon particular products and markets, and shedding its ties with particular industries and economies, by taking on a conglomerate structure and acquiring an international status. The modern business corporation, infinitely divisible, infinitely flexible, committed irrevocably to nothing but its own future, capable of unlimited expansion by way of growth or merger, safeguarded from hypertrophy by the competition of fellow Molochs, and by its own immunity from permanent attachments to places and things, its respectability as a semi-public institution assured by its combination of massive stability with resounding achievement, is beginning to enjoy all the advantages conferred by the solidity of the graven image without sacrificing any of those bestowed by the impalpable qualities of divinity, such as its indefinable nature and its unpredictable destiny.[6]

There was a time when even the sternest theology was bound to concede that, fundamentally, life was for love, and friendship, and laughter, and that work, apart from the doing of things that were a delight or an inspiration, was nothing but a necessary evil. Even Puritanism at its most misanthropic never attempted to do more than make the best of a bad job by claiming that the evil of work was a lesser good. Theology we have still. But it is theology with a difference. Secularized as political economy, its concern with larger issues debased by a passion for quantification into welfare economics, modern theology has become the science of the religion of number. The older theology stopped counting at three. Modern theology counts on. Work has therefore changed its status. Since it raises output and employment and hence the volume of things that can be counted, work is no longer a curse or an anodyne. It is now the supreme good. And the business corporation, the embodied symbol of modern productive might, is the incarnate deity of this modish religion.

In this looking-glass world process is reality; means are ends; and we are invited, if not positively charged, to dispense with morbid and futile preoccupation with anachronistic notions of civil liberty and private ease to the extent that such things hamper the growth, impair the health, or threaten the immortality of this holy presence.

The business corporation must be gorged with profits so as to be able to finance further expansion. If this means fabricating wants and inducing needs, then the consumer must submit, in the name of output, to a preposterous regimen which in the end will presumably leave him content to do without the necessities of life provided that he can be sure of its luxuries. But the consumer cannot buy without money, or acquire money without working. Accordingly leisure, the intoxicating power to command one's own time, once the promised reward for a life of virtue, later the visionary dream of social reformers, must be sacrificed to a factitious craving for things. Nor is leisure the sole, or even perhaps

[6] Several well-known writers have drawn attention to this phenomenon, which is perceptively examined by Edith T. Penrose, *The Theory of the Growth of the Firm*, Blackwell, 1959. See also: Robert T. Averitt, *The Dual Economy*, Norton, New York, 1968.

the chief casualty of this grotesque roundabout of compulsive getting and spending. As the delirium spreads the business corporation thrives and expands, creating an aggregation of financial and political power which makes it superior to everything else in the community except for other corporations of similar stature, and except for organized labour. The ordinary citizen is dwarfed and crushed by a process which nevertheless has no intrinsic meaning apart from the contribution it can make to his well-being. He cannot hope to control it by appealing to government, for government heeds only interests; and his interests as citizen, neighbour, and political equal of everyone else in the community, of whatever rank, quality, or degree, can only be expressed through his allegiance to one side or the other in a Baron's War fought principally over issues of pay and conditions of work.

In theory dissent can seek political redress: parliamentary candidature is open to all; the ballot is secret; suffrage universal. But ruthlessly efficient party organization and uncompromisingly strict party discipline have banished dissent from politics as effectually as the property franchise ever did, except for the speciously placid institutionalized animosities of parliamentary wrangle and exchange.

Consequently at the very moment when advanced technology has pointed the way to the conquest of famine, the defeat of epidemic disease, and the redemption of the race from its immemorial bondage to toilsome labour, a new feudalism emerges, in deadly menace to the integrity of the commonwealth and the independence and well-being of the individual, dedicated to the service of the god of cornucopia even as its predecessor in the Middle Ages was dedicated to the service of the god of war.

It is this religion of materialism, propagated with greatest fervour by the most dedicated of the enemies of Marxism, that pervades the intellectual atmosphere in which the economic historian does his work. It induces in him an acute susceptibility to the claims and blandishments of huge corporations and the keenest partiality for the colourful autocrats who created them. It is a religion which is repugnant to liberal values and incompatible with political good sense. Since it postulates energetic competition as the spur, and a due succession of zestful and aggressive managers as the agents, of triumphant expansion and continuous change, its doctrines are contradicted by every scrap of historical experience we possess as to the behaviour of over-mighty subjects who have it within their power to reduce government to compliant partnership and turn rivalry into sententious rotarianism.

But the glamour of present achievement and future promise sheds an irresistible retrospective glow upon the commercial and industrial empires of the past; and historians who owe it to the integrity of their craft to be neutral in such matters, and to their honour and dignity as citizens of a free society to refrain from doting admiration of persons and organizations whose chief claim to recognition is that they have made an outstanding contribution to the imperialism of the market-place, by succumbing to their magnetism, are betraying the future in the act of distorting our vision of the past.

7   Farmers' glory?

The industrial historian's doting admiration of big business is matched by the farming historian's deferential enthusiasm for the big estate. Modern observers of peasant farming, in regions where peasant farms operate side by side with European ones, have noted that peasant farms are not necessarily less efficient than European ones. They may look disorderly where European farms look trim. They may rely upon traditional methods where European farms exploit the latest techniques. But, for all that, they are not necessarily making less good use of scarce resources than the European farms are. Plantation managers with much capital invested and hired labour to pay for, set themselves to get a high yield per plant and per worker. Peasant farmers with little capital invested and no hired labour to pay for, set themselves to get a high yield per unit of surface area cultivated. With certain crops the big farmer has the edge over the small farmer in the development of better strains, or in the growing of superior grades. Sometimes the introduction of a new crop demands an investment the small farmer cannot afford because it entails organizing transport and marketing facilities on a scale which is beyond his means. Often enough the business of providing the facilities, or developing the better strains, has been made possible by co-operative effort, or by the effort of promoters with no commercial interest in farming. But once the thing is done, the big farmer enjoys few advantages which he can deny to his small competitors who, thenceforth, in so many regions, and with respect to so many crops, competes on more or less level terms with him.[1]

[1] Small, in this context, is extremely hard to define. In acreage, dairying, horticulture, arable, and pasture, have always had very different needs.
For the purpose of this chapter, however, the small farm means anything below the size that normally preoccupies the farming historian's thoughts.
Robert Loder, farming under 200 acres in early seventeenth-century

The historian, looking back over the centuries, cannot hope to rival the penetration of modern insights. Where the modern observer can watch the processes he is analysing, and compare the success achieved by those who use different methods of production, the historian is confined to records which are not only staggeringly deficient in volume, but also hopelessly inadequate in range. As if it were not handicap enough to have nothing remotely comparable with the kind of evidence which the modern observer has at his disposal, the historian suffers from the further disability of seeing the problems of farming through the eyes of the big farmer and the big estate-owner, to the detriment of the small man, for the simple reason that his records are chiefly the records kept by those who farmed or owned in a big way.

The deficiences of his records reinforce the historian's natural disposition to favour what is big and looks prosperous, and give comfort to his profound belief that there is a necessary connexion between size and efficiency. The modern observer may have concluded from his scrutiny of the commercial behaviour of any number of groups of peasant farmers that small farmers are perfectly capable of responding resourcefully to market opportunities. The societies to which such farmers belong may be infinitely less sophisticated and mature than the technologically commonplace but socially, politically, and intellectually advanced societies of later medieval and early modern Europe studied by historians of farming. Yet the commonest feature of writings upon European farming history is their facile disparagement of the small farmer, who is almost invariably depicted, after the manner of Arthur Young, a distinguished exponent of the caricature, as a cloddish imbecile with neither the means nor the skill, neither the will nor the foresight, to do more than float sluggishly with the tide when prices rose, and lie helplessly waterlogged in the shallows when they fell.

No doubt there were many times when social and demographic pressure reduced the small farmer's efforts as they reduced his hopes. But the centuries are no more equal in this respect than

Berkshire, is, perhaps, the pattern of the type. See G. E. Fussell (ed), *Robert Loder's Farm Accounts 1610–1620*, Camden Society, third series, vol. 53, 1936. For some unusually enlightening comments on modern peasant agriculture, see H. Myint, *Economic Theory and Development Policy*, Bell, 1967.

they are in any other. Nevertheless, modern surveys of English farming history, taking their cue from Arthur Young and his like, have the charm, if not the merit, of simplicity. The medieval landowner with his immense estates was a great thing; his tribulations in the later Middle Ages were a blight upon farming. The Tudor aristocracy never quite succeeded in supplying his place, though lesser men tried hard to do so, and the yeoman-farmer did his rugged best. English farming history, therefore, despite stalwart efforts recently made to plant landmarks in a spectral landscape, becomes a confusion of enclosures and open fields, small farmers and rapacious foreclosers, innovators and traditionalists, until the great families, the wealthy innovators, and the model farmers, resuming their traditional ascendancy, marched the farmers of England towards the triumphant achievements of the eighteenth and nineteenth centuries.

Views such as these create their own problems and involve their exponents in unavoidable contradictions. Historically speaking the big farm consisting of contiguous acres along the lines of an Australian sheep or a Canadian wheat farm was an anomaly in European conditions until comparatively recently. Many big farmers kept retinues of clerks whose papers have intrigued generations of historians. Usually, however, they were big farmers by dint of owning large estates, or occupying large tenancies carved out of such estates, which consisted of small, or fairly small farms, each of which had to be supervised by a manager, if it was not run by a tenant. Consequently until the technological developments of the nineteenth century made it a feasible business proposition, the large estate had few advantages over the small farm that were not nullified by the administrative costs of running a big but scattered organization.

Most of the land of England has, in fact, always been worked by small farmers. In the feudal centuries when the manorial estate, whatever its size, was nothing but a congeries of small farms, the villeins were, in effect, simply tenant-farmers, paying rent in kind and in service for their holdings, as well as in money, instead of paying it exclusively in money as farmers did later. With most of the land portioned out in penny packets what could a reforming medieval landlord do but set a trifling example of prudent husbandry and hope to be copied? If there were achievements in these centuries, then the small farmer has surely earned the credit for them no less than the big. But modern writers do not relish the thought that great consequences can flow from the unco-ordinated but uniform response to market opportunities of thousands of families which were distinguished neither by birth nor income from the common run of mankind, and urge their readers to share their unreasoning approbation for the big farmer by reserving the credit for whatever was accomplished in medieval times for the cumbersome bureaucratic organizations whose office routines they understand so well and retail at such length.

Accordingly, when they have to explain later developments, loyalty to consistency of argument takes precedence over loyalty to facts. In the later Middle Ages the big landlord surrendered his home farms to tenants, whose domination of the English farming scene was thenceforth undisputed. By the late fourteenth century, therefore, nearly all the wool exported from England, whether raw or made up into cloth, was grown by small or fairly small tenant-farmers. Enormous quantities went abroad, then and later. But current orthodoxy teaches, as it must do, that in the later Middle Ages the peasant-farmer was dedicated to a torpid life of self-sufficiency. Later still, in the sixteenth century, when England exported huge quantities of cloth and scarcely any wool at all, the wool content of exports was not very much greater than it had been two centuries earlier. But current orthodoxy teaches that immense reforms in husbandry were necessary, of which the bigger farmer was the pioneer, or at any rate the moving spirit, before this extraordinary feat could be accomplished. At neither period can we know the size of the home market for wool, apart from knowing that the late medieval peasant lived well and presumably used more wool than his sixteenth-century successors, who lived exceedingly poorly mainly because there were so many of them.

Between the sixteenth and nineteenth centuries, farming methods improved and output rose as a growing population and—for about one hundred years after the mid-seventeenth century—a substantial export trade in corn were sustained, apparently without loss of nutrition, by a more or less stable area of cultivation; and in the nineteenth century, by a more or less stable farming population. The logic of these developments requires that in the course of these centuries the small farmer should have gone to the wall. The process may have been slow, retarded by all the considerations that made landlords refrain from foreclosure, and poor farmers delay their move into better-paid work. Nevertheless improvements which, over the centuries, failed to knock out the small farmer would seem to argue a capacity to make skilful use of available resources which might not surprise a modern observer of peasant farming in Malaya and West Africa, but could not fail to confound those who follow Arthur Young in execrating the small farmer and all his works. Historians of farming have, therefore, proclaimed the ultimate decline of the small farmer, and his impending dispossession by larger and more efficient rivals, almost as regularly as their colleagues have hailed the rise of the middle classes.

But the small farmer, despite the strenuous efforts of historians to suppress him, displaying an incorrigibly perverse tenacity, obstinately refuses to disappear. The latest writer to tackle him has had to concede that even as late as the 1880s farms of less than 100 acres still occupied over one-fifth of the acreage reported on.[2] A different classification of the returns, which included farms of rather more than 100 acres in the lowest category, might have given an even more striking proof of the persistence, if not the vitality, of the smaller farm in an age in which capital was beginning to tell decisively, even in farming : for nearly half the farms in the kingdom were to be found in the next classification.

The truth would seem to be that size has had very little to do with efficiency, at least until recent times, and that the active peasant farmer, however small his tenancy, and the ambitious landlord, however modest his inheritance, have always managed to better themselves at the expense of ineffectual neighbours and rivals. On the whole success leaves a more enduring mark than failure; and energy and ambition are therefore rewarded with a measure of immortality. Hence, perhaps, the impression of ever-burgeoning wealth and ever-increasing size that historians have so

[2] James Caird, *English Agriculture in 1850–51* (with a new introduction by G. E. Mingay), Cass, 1968, p. xxv, citing J. H. Clapham, *An Economic History of Modern Britain*, vol. 2, Cambridge University Press, 1932, pp. 263–4. The 100 acre classification includes the type of farm with, perhaps, one or two virgates, which did so much in the later Middle Ages to produce the output that kept corn prices as consistently low as they then were, and wool production so high. See F. G. Davenport, *The Economic History of a Norfolk Manor*, Cambridge University Press, 1906, Cass, 1967.

gratefully seized upon and made much of. But as always in such matters, the forces making for size were, in fact, opposed by powerful countervailing forces. The reservoir was replenished by those who fell back as quickly as it was depleted by those who rose above their circumstances. Marriage, litigation and other forms of social pressure dissolved property complexes as well as augmenting them. The Reformation intervened to break up larger estates, perhaps, than it created. And rising prices regularly multiplied the number of tenancies as scarcity drove up land values, just as falling prices did the opposite.

It was perhaps just as well that the forces of disintegration worked so remorselessly upon the pattern of farms; for there is much to be said for the view that the larger aggregations of land were often a positive menace to the efficiency of farming. Farming profits have always been uncertain; consequently farming income has always been more expeditiously improved by efforts devoted to the acquisition of more farms, provided that the terms were right, than it could ever have been by efforts devoted to the tiresome rituals of better farming practice. Until recently, moreover, land conferred social standing, its efficacy as an agent of social advancement increasing disproportionately with the amount acquired. Hence the incentive to farm well has inevitably been weaker, especially at the higher end of the social scale, than the incentive to farm more extensively. Those who ran the bigger estates and farmed the bigger tenancies have always been keener students of the marriage market, therefore, than of any of the more prosaic markets that might have claimed their professional attention. At the top incurable extravagance has always added a certain piquancy to the study: for the aristocratic classes have invariably been hard up, whether they lived in the reign of Henry III or George III. Hence it is quite wrong to see those who ran the biggest farming complexes as businessmen. They were not, in the least, the rural counterparts of the great captains of commerce and industry. Until industrialization destroyed them, except as an incongruous remnant, they were primarily socialites or statesmen, choosing their chief advisers for their legal and political skills rather than for their knowledge of farming, and either running their farms as showpieces, or using them as counters, or pledges, in schemes of litigation, matrimony, or politics.

I

Some of these men spent immense sums of money upon improvements. And much was done for English farming by those who had the will and the means to spend on this scale. But it was yet another case of burning down the house in order to roast a pig. In farming, as in war, good came out of a vast diversion of resources from ordinary productive employment; but the cost was high; in this case because the improvers did not always understand what they were about. How often, indeed, was theirs the story of the estate of Mr Horace Pendyce in Galsworthy's *The Country House*! 'Originally a fine property let in smallish holdings to tenants who, having no attention bestowed on them, did very well and paid excellent rents, it was now farmed on model lines at a slight loss.' Such improvements were variously inspired : paid tribute, perhaps, to warm hearts rather than to cool heads; flattered self-esteem; flaunted wealth; sustained social pretensions; owed much to mulish adherence to proven orthodoxies subsequently perpetuated by being written into the leases of tenants; and often enough reflected the kind of bad advice that delayed English progress, in the nineteenth century, along the road travelled so rapidly by the farmers of Denmark.

But if improvement, as imposed upon the countryside by the bigger owners and farmers, did so much less than it is reputed to have done to raise the standards of English farming, rising prices did less still. In the thirteenth and sixteenth centuries, and possibly at times in the seventeenth and eighteenth centuries, rising prices wrought havoc with farming by encouraging the bigger farmers to take life even more easily than they were habitually disposed to do. Rising rents and rising prices took the hazard and effort out of their lives. This tempted them to do little more than safeguard their incomes by employing clerks to see that they were actually paid what was their due; and increase their incomes, not so much by taking thought about farming practices, as by splitting tenancies into smaller units, so as to keep pace with a growing but poorer population, and by reducing the length of leases, so as to keep pace with the opportunities provided by rising rents.

Meanwhile the small farmer survived the vicissitudes of the centuries; adapting his routines to changing conditions; responding to market forces with as much alacrity as any groundnuts or cotton farmer; taking advantage of innovations when they suited his needs, or fitted into the pattern of relative scarcities to which he had to reconcile all his other activities; lapsing into boorish and slovenly lassitude when he could, as readily as his betters did; making mistakes, no doubt, but raising the general level of farming practice, by way of infinitesimal adjustments, as and when opportunity offered.

As a rule the small farmer left no record for the historian to scrutinize except for the improvements in output and productivity that all could see. And these he achieved without spending lavishly upon research and development or investing heavily in ambitious capital projects. Capital was something that important reforms sometimes required. But it is impossible to turn the pages of Caird's classic survey of English farming in the mid-nineteenth century without being reminded of the exhortations of earlier reformers of husbandry, some of them far back in English history, and of their common theme that momentous things can be accomplished without great expense, by taking thought, by attending carefully to matters which it is easy to scamp or neglect, and by making small but significant changes in the everyday routines of the farm.

If output and productivity rose in the eighteenth and nineteenth centuries it was partly, possibly it was mainly, because the smaller farmers of England, no less capable of responding to market forces than the peasants who were soon to grow so much of the world's internationally-traded supplies of staple foodstuffs and raw materials, put into practice the simple precepts of good husbandry, some of them known for centuries, which had been universally disregarded for long periods when there was no incentive to apply them.

Historians, however, love a hero, particularly an aristocratic hero who can be depicted as living according to the canons of *noblesse oblige*. At present, therefore, they are busy manufacturing an Arcadian idyll set in the English countryside, much like the one that American historians once manufactured for the benefit of the southern aristocrat. According to this idyll, the aristocratic English landowner touched with chivalry all the relationships of a richly various life. His chivalry, however, like his contribution to farming practice, was surely bought at a devastating price. It was the chivalry of the autocrat, whose imperious, indeed feudal, control of every aspect of the social life of the countryside sapped the independence and stifled the enterprise of the smaller men upon whom so much of the prosperity of farming depended. When spurned or questioned, it was a chivalry which was capable of the most implacably vindictive ferocity. And like the chivalry of feudalism itself it made the nicest distinctions between those whom it acknowledged and served, and those whom it utterly ignored or repudiated. It did not scruple, therefore, to subordinate the well-being of the nation to the interests of a class, and of a system of dependence. Vital questions of farming policy concerning wages, prices, tenure, and the like, it settled on terms which moved Acton to declare that almost everything done for the good of the people had been done since the aristocratic landowners had lost their monopoly of political power.[3]

The small farmers who got better prices and paid lower wages than they might have done but for the collusive arrangements made by their aristocratic betters, no doubt welcomed many of their actions, particularly, perhaps, after the Restoration when export bounties were added to their arsenal of commercial weapons. The ordinary consumer, however, cannot have watched the various attempts made by these interests to manipulate the terms upon which the basic resources of the community were to be exploited, with anything but foreboding. Some of these attempts were self-defeating as caustic observers like Adam Smith were quick to point out. But the class that controlled parliament as it controlled the social and economic life of the countryside could afford to blunder over trifles. And the consumer could take no comfort from tactical errors committed by men who might sometimes take farming seriously and make a commercial success of it, or experiment with new farming techniques and discover something worth having, but whose purposes were essentially social and political purposes, and who used their wealth and influence to promote these purposes and not, except incidentally, to make profits out of farming by making the best economic use they could of the scarce resources at their disposal.

The effect of a system which offered the most influential section of the community every possible inducement to ignore the market, and every possible temptation to impose its arrogant conservatism upon a deferential tenantry, was to slacken the faltering pace of change by conferring the authority of birth and rank

[3] Herbert Paul (ed), *Letters of Lord Acton*, Allen, 1904, p. 94.

upon the pernicious habit of sticking to time-honoured routines, and by inculcating servility in those whom social and economic dependence had in any case made wary of exercising initiative in farming matters. Historians who are impressed by the contributions to farming that we owe to the big farmer and the improving landowner give them full credit for their efforts without reckoning the price that farming had to pay for their intermittent benefactions. It is always easier to recognize a concrete benefit than to allow for an equally real but intangible cost. The case for the big men therefore goes by default. If farming made only sluggish progress at many periods when the need was plainly for rapid change, historians content themselves with the reflexion, against all the evidence of anthropologists and economists, that farmers are notoriously suspicious of innovation. And the story of farming is told in terms of bold initiatives and portentous investments when the truth might be better served if it were told instead in terms of markets rigged, land supplies restricted by entail, tentative enterprise crushed, small but significant opportunities obstructed, timid attempts to surmount vexatious obstacles vehemently rebuffed, and consumers held to ransom everywhere, and at all times, for the sake of the social dignity, the political ascendancy, and the military glory, of small groups of men and women whose chief distinction seems to be that they have invariably taken more out of the community than they have ever contributed to it.

In ages when the incomes spent by consumers had generally been earned by selling farm products, only the landless consumer with nothing but his labour to sell was utterly at the mercy of the major farming interests. At such periods the discomfiture of the consumer was, perforce, very much less complete than an aristocratically controlled dispensation could make it once society had advanced to the point where commerce and industry, administration and the learned professions, occupied substantial minorities for some, if not most, of their working lives. The extent to which skills were multiplied and differentiated in the crafts and professions that emerged as society advanced, and the level of well-being that prevailed in them, depended very greatly upon the prosperity of farming; for farmers and those who lived upon farming incomes were for long the best customers for such skills. And the middle-class element in these crafts and professions was

perfectly capable of protecting itself from the untoward consequences of farm prices which were higher than they might have
been in the absence of market imperfections sedulously promoted
and maintained by the ruling landed interests, by itself devising
and enforcing codes of restrictive practices which raised rates of
reward for services rendered, well above the competitive level.
But there were long, and often swollen, retinues of workers in
these occupations, who were utterly incapable of protecting themselves in this way. These, as society achieved greater and greater
differentiation of skills, joined in ever-rising numbers the ranks of
the farm-labourers who, as consumers, found themselves with less
money to spare for other purchases than they might have had,
because farm products, and the things that were made out of farm
products, cost more than they would have done in circumstances
of competition. But the consumer is an obscure personage, without organization and without influence, and therefore not some-
one whom the historian really wants to know.

8 The professions and the unions

The consumer takes as low a place in the economic historian's hierarchy of values as the ordinary voter does in the political historian's. In each case the person for whose sake the whole business of politics, and all the processes of making, growing and trading, are supposed to be carried on, is treated as if he were no more than the residuary legatee of the system, instead of its principal beneficiary with every right to his say in how he is to be benefited. In economic affairs it is easy to see how this has come about. Everyone may be a consumer; but not every consumer is a recipient of income from work or property; and those who are take care to give precedence to their interests as earners over their interests as consumers. From their own point of view they have undoubtedly got their priorities right : for in the long run wealth and social preferment go to those who can organize importunity to greatest effect. This means organizing the trade or the profession, not the consumer, who is a nebulous abstraction less amenable to organization than any other group in the community. And the most successfully organized interests then get the best press as well as the best results; for the historian gladly takes the winner at his own valuation.

Until recently, even in the richest communities, life was so hard for most people, and contracted to so narrow a compass of needs, that the clashes and triumphs of organized interest may well have appeared to be as remote from their immediate cares as the legendary affrays of the gods. But they were not in the least remote. Poverty was the common lot because resources were scarce; and they were scarce, generally speaking, not only because population growth tended to exceed their capacity to sustain any such growth without stringency, but also because society was invariably organized for the benefit of controlling minorities which settled questions of wealth distribution very much on their own terms, and hence invariably exercised a determining influence upon what should be grown, or made, or built, or spent upon colonial adventure or war.

In short, the direction that social pressure compelled the community to take was not chosen by the ordinary people who were compelled to take it; and since such pressure meant diverting resources from the production of the essential things that ordinary people most urgently required, for the sake of purposes which often meant little or nothing to them, it may not have been the direction that the vast majority of them would have taken if they had been able to choose.

At various periods of history change may have been very rapid. But speed is unavailing when the direction is wrong; and historians who applaud rapid change are betrayed by their predilection for the spectacular into extolling changes which may have added exceedingly little to the real prosperity of society. Moreover, these changes came at a cost to the ordinary consumer which, because of restrictive practices, is likely to have been out of all proportion to the value of what was achieved, even granting for the moment that what was achieved was what ought to have been achieved.

No doubt the deflection imparted to the course and speed of economic change by social forces such as these was not to be compared in momentousness with the vast influence of impersonal forces such as human fecundity. Yet it would be wrong to underestimate it. Modern economic development has encompassed miraculous changes in many countries north of the equator and in some to the south of it. But it takes little sophistication to perceive that the most striking gains for the ordinary consumer have usually come where unrestricted access to rich and abundant resources has been guaranteed by central government action in opposing protection, as in Britain, or inter-state tariffs, as in America; or where countries, such as Sweden and Switzerland, have learned to devote to the arts of peace the concentrated thought and energy that others have devoted to the arts of war.

Large claims have always been made for the maturity of judgment, and the civic virtues, exercised by ruling groups with every incentive to spread the notion that there was more to their ascendancy than ancient riches or privileged access to the seat of power. But it takes a very accommodating nature to see the history of any class, or party, or interest, or majority, in such terms. And if inequalities of wealth and income are not justifiable on grounds of inherited skills, then they are justifiable, presumably, only when they are functional, reflecting real scarcities of skills, capital, raw materials and enterprise. But inequalities of income have never been confined to what has been made necessary by the elemental dilemma of finite resources and infinite needs. Inequality has always been the crucial factor in social organization, fostered at all levels of society for the sake of its beneficiaries, without the least regard for the well-being of colleagues, associates, social equals, or the community as a whole. Industrialization which has done so much for a minority of the world's population, has proved itself to be as fully compatible as any of its predecessors, with systems of inequality which range from something not far short of slavery at one extreme, through the exploitation of the unpaid and underpaid work of women and other depressed groups, to the conspiracies against the public interest practised by the leading commercial and industrial groups at the other extreme.

Prominent amongst these engines of inequality are the professions, and their junior counterparts, the trades unions. The historian can scarcely fail to approve of the professions. With their honourable traditions, ancient dignity, and impeccable distinction of achievement, they fulfil all his most cherished ideals. But he has other reasons for thinking well of them. He is himself a member of one of the most illustrious of the professions, a product of one of the most arduous and prolonged of all the apprenticeship systems. He knows, therefore, how to value professionalism; and when a new profession acquires its charter of incorporation, welcomes it unreservedly to the fold. He knows that professionalism establishes the presumption of a modest level of competence in the work of anyone who has passed the appropriate tests in youth, and has supplemented training with experience, or at least, if learning from experience were beyond him, has, at any rate, managed to remember enough of what he was taught to see him through without disaster or ignominy. And he knows that something of the *esprit de corps* of the profession, which training also attempts to instill, will probably strengthen even the infirmest purpose, when the professional man is tempted to betray professional standards of work or conduct. He should know from experience, if not from the mordant pages of *Microcosmo-graphia Academica*, that no one understands better than the professional man how to block reform and obstruct change.[1] And he may be uneasily aware that things change more quickly outside the professions than within them. But his keen appreciation of the value of the professions leads him to take the most sympathetically indulgent view of their shortcomings, and even to look upon some of these as merits.

He has, of course, read his Adam Smith. But whenever he does so, it is out of respect for a masterpiece of literature, if not as an act of piety to the father of modern economic analysis : for nothing of the radicalism of that revolutionary mind lingers in his. And when he passes the professions in review, Adam Smith is back on the bookshelf, instead of beside him, open on his desk. Consequently, when he sees the glittering prizes that rewarded professional success, it never occurs to him to suggest that the prizes were glittering because the market had been rigged. The professions, however, have always managed to compound the intrinsic complexities of their respective crafts by devising and making compulsory a series of wholly unnecessary ritualistic and linguistic difficulties, by introducing fresh difficulties without dispensing with existing ones, and by allowing these complexities to run riot in a multiplicity of recondite specialisms, between which encroachment, even by fellow members of the profession concerned, was either discountenanced or expressly forbidden. In such ways as these, the professions have generally managed to guarantee the market for professional services by making it virtually impossible for the layman to tackle a variety of important problems for himself even when the law did not in fact preclude him from doing so. And the historian, who might have been expected to know better, can apparently see no harm in what they did.

One of the principal duties of the professions has always been to prepare beginners for their careers. The rewards of professional work have invariably attracted throngs of applicants to the professions. They would have attracted greater throngs than they did, but for the ban on women, which kept the professions as a male reserve for so long, and but for the insistence by the professions

[1] F. M. Cornford, *Microcosmographia Academica*, Bowes & Bowes, 1908.

upon a variety of social and educational accomplishments as necessary qualifications for entry, which had the intended effect of shutting out large numbers of those with aptitude enough for the real work of the professions, but with neither the background nor the upbringing that were required. Those who were not disqualified by sex or class were subjected to a course of training whose most remarkable feature was its determination to inculcate things that it was either unnecessary to know or pointless to memorize. The rigmarole prolonged the training, however, and the training, which had very conveniently but quite fortuitously provided cheap labour for the professions while it lasted, then gave the professions their final opportunity to reduce entry to an absolute minimum, when it was over, by providing them with the excuse for a qualifying or competitive examination.

Those who passed these examinations were not always better off, however, than those who failed them. So successful were the professions in raising to the limit the highest rewards of professional work, that they attracted many more applicants to the professions than they could decently exclude from their ranks. Inevitably, therefore, particularly in teaching and the church, they admitted many more than they could support in comfort and dignity, and disappointed more hopes than they could fulfil. Those at the bottom formed an educated proletariat, whether they had passed their examinations or not : Langland is, perhaps, the most famous English exemplar of the type. Many of them would have done far better for themselves if they had got a trade. But by the time that their hopes were dashed it was usually too late to make a change, even if it had been socially possible for them to have done so.

The professions were as unperturbed by demands for reform made by those who had failed to make a success of their professional careers, as they were to demands for redress made by those who had been the victims of a measure of professional incompetence or misconduct which fell short of flagrant and sensational criminality. The professional bodies that presided over the usages upon which the strength of the professions depended, also heard the complaints that were lodged against members; and in both capacities set the honour and dignity of the professions high above the unseemly remonstrances of those who were dissatisfied with their workings. As a tribute to human ingenuity in contriving a system which combined the maximum scope for exploiting the unfortunate consumer with the minimum risk of being undercut, the professions were probably unsurpassed.

The professions did not have things all their own way. There were unlicensed dealers, who were prepared to do things that the professionals would not do, or to do things in ways that the professionals would not do them. And new professions arose, as accountancy did, to take work away from an existing profession, as well as to do work which had not been done by a profession before. Interlopers such as these brought a refreshingly energetic and creative originality to bear upon professionalism, rebuking the sterility and outraging the orthodoxy of those whose routines had stood the test of time mainly because time had never been allowed to have much effect upon them. But the historian is seldom heartened by their efforts to break the stranglehold of professional exclusiveness and aloofness to public need. When they succeed he is intensely appreciative of their qualities and their services. During the struggles that precede victory, however, his natural desire to back the winner is at odds with his fellow-feeling for a profession at bay; and in exposing the shortcomings of established professional organizations, he ostentatiously refrains from drawing up a general indictment against them which, like Adam Smith's, could all too easily be turned against the profession to which he himself belongs.

This is a more serious matter than most, because the professions have never had much difficulty in holding the community to ransom for essential services. Even when *laissez-faire* dominated politics, when the trade unions had to fight in order to establish for themselves a position in society which was anything better than the barest sufferance, *laissez-faire* utterly failed to liberalize the professions. Naturally there were excellent reasons why the politically influential classes which took such pride in the efficient productive and distributive system that served and rewarded them all so handsomely once industrialization had got into its stride, should be content with professions which changed with the times but changed far less than they remained the same. The professions were, after all, their undisputed preserves, providing them with employment in which they could hope to enjoy lucrative and dignified ease. Reforming them thoroughly would have meant an end to all that. It would have meant making them as capable of giving quick, cheap and effective service as any shopkeeper was, once transport, banking and the telegraph had linked the continents and enabled him to satisfy his customer's idlest whim. It would have meant lifting the barriers and admitting the hordes. It would have meant simplifying cherished professional procedures, and reducing to a minimum the content of professional skill requisite for the dispatch of any particular item of professional business, from the simplest to the most complex. Reforming the professions, however, would have had even graver consequences than these. It would have meant reforming the substance of which each profession was at once the guardian, the servant, and the beneficiary.

Quick, cheap and effective service is of no use to a man whose problems are not catered for by those who provide it. Hence reforming the professions would have brought momentous consequences in its train. It would have forced the doctors, as it once tried to force the church, to pay serious attention to the needs of the great majority of ordinary people, instead of allowing them to get away with devoting themselves as exclusively and assiduously as they did, to the vapours and infirmities of the rich.[2] And the repercussions of the reform of the legal profession could have been more far-reaching than almost anything else achieved in a century of radical change.

The law's delays reflected the conjunction of an antiquated profession with an antiquated system of legal administration. The profession and the system were in fact nothing but two aspects of the same thing. And if the public were to have prompt and effective legal redress, and were to get it as cheaply as it was finding that it could get its food and its clothing, its household goods, its travel, and its news, then the lawyers would have had to do what everyone else had done. They would have had to gear their earnings to high turn-over and low prices. Low prices would have necessitated their simplifying every process that was not scrapped

[2] When the church neglected its flocks in the Middle Ages, it did so because absentee impropriators put incompetent clerks in charge of the parishes. When the church neglected them later, it was because the middle classes returned to the vicarages and rectories, only to conduct services over the heads of their flocks, and live lives that were utterly remote from theirs. See, for example, K. S. Inglis, *Churches and the Working Classes in Victorian England*, Routledge & Kegan Paul, 1963.

as superfluous, and high turn-over, providing what a mass-market of ordinary litigants required of the law.

At this point the problem of professional reform ceases to be, in any sense, a coterie issue, and gets caught up in one of the gravest social issues of modern times : the issue of equality before the law. Until very recently the doctrine of equality before the law meant, in practice, the equality of the moneyed classes before a law which centuries of legislation and precedent had moulded into a form which suited the problems that moneyed people encountered in their daily round. Those without fairly substantial means the law knew only as debtors, defaulters, intruders, vagabonds, agitators, cut-purses, and the like, and the profession knew scarcely at all. Money alone unlocked the door to justice. The law could not help anyone too poor to initiate an action, or meet the costs of his own defence. Nor could it see things from his point of view, and in the interests of parity of treatment, offer him the protection that corresponded to his needs. On the contrary, parliament discriminated against him; and the courts were ill-disposed towards him. But with the best will in the world, the courts could not possibly have compensated for absence of legislation, or for antagonistic legislation, when they lacked that daily familiarity with the problems of life and work as they presented themselves to labourers, shop assistants, outdoor and factory workers, domestic servants, and others in like circumstances, which they could have acquired only if a miracle had happened, and those who knew the courts only from the angle of the dock, could have had their predicaments vividly and sympathetically dramatized by the skilful advocacy of a succession of professional lawyers of the highest calibre, whose services normally commanded the highest fees.

Comprehensive reform of the legal system would have changed all that. It would have provided law to suit the needs of the humblest litigant with an action to bring. It would have multiplied the number of courts, abolished the undemanding ritual of the Law Term and the spacious pageantry of the Assize Circuit, in favour of continuous session, and provided the means whereby all manner of problems which had been settled hitherto, if they had been settled at all, by informal courts of one sort or another, or by administrative courts, could have had the benefit of judgment by law. It would have enormously simplified procedures, and enormously reduced professional costs. In short, comprehensive legal reform would have placed at the disposal of the ordinary citizen the means with which to seek redress for the injuries he had suffered at the hands of those whom the law's grotesque inadequacies, as well as the law's costs, and the law's delays, had shielded from litigation and punishment.

The ramifications of legal reform, in this sense, are so momentous that no parliament has ever dared to contemplate them. The interests of one of the most powerful sections of the community have always stood four-square against any movement in the direction of such reform. And the historian, who is so ready to praise the law and its institutions, who traces their majestic evolution with such deferential enthusiasm, who cannot, or will not, conceive that the community could have paid an outrageous price for the crazy structure that wealth raised in honour of privilege, helps to fortify the resistance of all who oppose radical reform, by investing the law and its institutions with a spurious sanctity. Yet the importance of radical reform for the future of liberal democracy cannot be exaggerated. Nor would it be too much to say that if reform in this comprehensive sense had ever been carried through the trades union movement would have lost the main impetus of its tremendous growth.

We have come to see trade union development as the courageous and inspiring response of labour to the risks, strains, and dangers, of industrialization. The central hero of trade union history is the forlorn and pathetically broken figure of the urban and industrialized working man. As heroes go, the working man, with his cheerless background and sombre prospects, wasted, crippled in body if not in mind, hopelessly out-manoeuvred, with the odds stacked overwhelmingly against him, tragically beaten and subdued by an arrogant and invulnerable foe, makes a deeper and more complex appeal than any masterful conqueror fulfilling his destiny in stupendous triumph and unexampled catastrophe. Accordingly the story of trades union development is a success story with a difference. It is the story of how the poor and the oppressed have inherited the earth. We are, therefore, invited by those who tell it to rejoice when the trades unions win a famous victory, to share their vexation and bitterness when they suffer a reversal, and to honour and respect them when they achieve a status which exempts them from the rule of law. And indeed there is much to be said for this reaction to the march of events. If the trades unions developed beyond the point where they were merely voluntary associations of like-minded men and women dedicated to the betterment of their conditions of work, they did so in a society which had mobilized all the resources of law and politics against the working man. Problems of contractual relationships at work and in the home, which the law had neglected or circumvented, the profession was incapable of handling, and the courts could scarcely comprehend, had to be thrashed out in other places by men who were not trained to the work, and in circumstances in which bargaining power had, perforce, usurped the place that belonged, by right, to the impartial arbitrament of the courts. The working man needed the trade union to protect his legal rights for him, to extend and define rights which the law had failed to provide for him, and to be eternally vigilant on his behalf, just as he needed the quack with his nostrums when he was ill. In both cases restrictions upon the free development of professional practice had made it impossible for those without substantial means to turn to the professional classes for help in moments of crisis.

The truth about the trades unions, however, is not to be extricated without much difficulty from the pathos in which it is buried. The contribution of the trades unions to the working-class struggle against poverty and oppression has undoubtedly been outstanding. But their greatest contribution was not, perhaps, the one for which they get most credit. Poverty does, indeed, invite oppression, and is often the result of it. Hence poverty and oppression are indissolubly linked in radical political thinking about the working classes. But poverty is also the inevitable result of a scarcity of resources which redistribution of income may be able to mitigate but cannot possibly dispel. Nothing is easier than to confuse these factors and denounce oppression for creating the hardship and privation that scarcity of resources will inexorably impose upon any population which grows more quickly than it can form capital. And when conditions improve, it is often irresistibly tempting to use the improvements as a stick to beat the oppressors with, by claiming for triumphant working-class militancy, advances in welfare which are due, more often than not, to profound changes in economic circumstances.

Looking back over something less than a century of reliably

quantifiable information, it is tolerably clear from the massive work done by the statisticians that the rising living standards enjoyed by the vast majority of the population have, in fact, owed much less to redistribution than to the increasing productivity of farming, commerce, and industry. It would be wrong to conclude from the statistics, however, that working-class militancy gained comparatively little because there was comparatively little for it to gain. The constitutional historian, intent upon his beguiling evolutionary theme of progressive emancipation, may be content to disregard the extent to which, until recently, the machinery of law, administration, and government, by turns ignored and crushed the ordinary citizen, or disbarred him from its workings. But a more disinterested observer surely cannot fail to see working-class militancy as a mortifying reflection upon the constitution. And in the struggle to reduce the distance between the classes by removing the hindrances that thwarted the freedom and independence of the large majority of the population, and checked its economic advancement, none fought more strenuously or tirelessly than those who led the trades union movement. It was here, perhaps, that the trades unions did their finest work, by organizing informed and articulate dissent, and by helping to rouse and shame the landed and professional classes whose more thoughtful and sensitive members had already had their aversion to measures of reform undermined by reports and pressures emanating from quarters of unexceptionable respectability and unimpeachable authority.

This was no mere battle of movement in which adversaries dislodged one another from position after position without either side gaining permanent advantage from its efforts. Statistics of the course of income distribution cannot reckon changes in the climate of opinion which made influential people compunctuous about employers who bullied and exploited, laws which excluded and oppressed, and public controversy which kept social issues of tremendous moment out of politics. Striking things were accomplished; and the trades unions, though weak, and poor, and often at odds with one another; holding together, between them, a movement which, even at its peak before the First World War, succeeded in enrolling less than a quarter of the wage-earning population; nevertheless contributed more to the improvement of the social, political, and working conditions of the people they

K

stood for, than historians, particularly constitutional historians, care to give them credit for.

When they tried to raise wages they had less success. Their members belonged to a class which was numerous, relatively unskilled, largely ignorant of alternatives to the employment that was thrust upon it, and more or less immobile. Their adversaries, the employers, and behind them the financiers, were rich, well-informed, politically active and influential, and perfectly at liberty to transfer funds for new capital formation from industry to industry, and from region to region, and to export it should better opportunities present themselves elsewhere in the world. Moreover a thousand expedients lay to the employer's hand with which he could restore the rate of return on scarce resources by altering factor proportions so as to offset the nominal gains made as a result of trades union action.

When wage-earners were paid less, at the margin, than the value of what they did or made, trades unions could raise wages without provoking the retaliation of employers. Hence the widespread impression that unions were more successful at the start than subsequently. In other circumstances, however, the basic weakness of the trade union position meant that their manoeuvres in the battle for higher wages were met, more or less successfully, by the counter-measures of their adversaries.

Some gains were consolidated; for the unions were quick to learn from the professions, whose conspiracies in restraint of trade they strove to emulate. Unlike the professions, they were in no position to combine the loudest protestations of devotion to the public interest with the shrewdest manipulation of the market for their services; or to contrive, as the professions did, to incorporate the last refinements of restrictionism in a form which actually enhanced their reputation as guardians of the public interest and custodians of standards of competence, instead of destroying it. They could never hope to do as well as the professions had done. Everything was against them. They closed the shop, however, even though they could rarely restrict entry. They defined the boundaries of their respective occupations with punctilious exactitude, even though differentiating the processes of their crafts, as a profession might have done, was beyond them. They worked a conventional day, at a conventional, or at any rate an agreed pace, and long demurred, in many occupations, before they would work with any but conventional tools. Their greatest triumph was to secure a privileged status in the community so commanding that it drove one exasperated critic to complain that it gave them the same sort of advantage in wage-bargaining as a man might have in selling his house, if the law permitted him, in dealing with a potential buyer, to conspire with other house-owners so as to avoid being undersold, deprive the potential buyer of the opportunity to look for a better bargain, cut him off from all normal intercourse with society, and boycott his business until he agreed to buy at the seller's price.[3]

Such stratagems as these are naturally deplored by those historians who profess to see, in the corporate life of the medieval gild, not a decorous swindle, but a wholesome and refreshing manifestation of the medieval spirit of service; and in the activities of the professional associations which have done so much for the prestige and material well-being of the middle-class service trades, not a screen for self-interest, but an inspiring record of devotion to the highest ideals of social responsibility. But by wielding their coercive powers to good effect the trades unions have had great success in raising money wages; and success can never be denied its accolade. Hence even the most curmudgeonly enemy of organized labour has had to find a place of honour for a movement which has, apparently, accomplished so much.

In doing this, however, the enemies of trade unionism have been as mistaken as its friends. With conspicuous exceptions the victories won in the fight for higher money wages have been eroded subsequently, and even lost, as prices rose to restore the previous balance. And for the rest, the struggles of the trades unions have all too often degenerated into an anarchy of mutual spoliation in which relative advantage mattered more than rates of pay, and in which the triumphs of one moment were snatched away by predatory rivals at the next.

Life consists of moments; and any advantage, however brief, is better than none. Consequently unions which contend for prizes they cannot hope to keep are no more recklessly foolhardy, unscrupulously opportunistic, or short-sighted, than businessmen who take a profit when they see one, politicians who come upon their opponents bathing and make off with their clothes, or indeed any-

<hr>

[3] F. A. Hayek, *The Constitution of Liberty*, Routledge & Kegan Paul, 1960, p. 506, note 17, citing the words of E. H. Chamberlin.

one at all who steals a march upon those with whom he is dealing. In the light of retrospective prescience it may be obvious that certain policies have proved to be too clever by half, and that the permanent interests of the parties concerned would have been better served by the renunciation of opportunities which were so avidly seized upon. At the time, however, the choice is always between a tangible advantage which none can deny, and an hypothetical benefit which a thousand mischances can readily frustrate. And success is always infinitely easier to justify than failure is to excuse.

Moreover, as with so many problems, the ostensible ground of conflict was rarely the real cause of contention.

> The traveller who visits an old battlefield can never fully understand what its various natural features meant to the combatants. He is shown, perhaps, a rocky ridge which is called the key of the position. He reads that it was taken and repurchased on hard terms more than once during the day. But it is an ordinary object in the landscape. A dozen such eminences have been seen during the morning's ride. Was it really so important? Were the fortunes of kingdoms actually for some hours involved in the possession of those few acres of rank grass and scattered stone? As he stands serenely on ground where once the bravest soldier hardly dared to crawl, he can scarcely believe it. Yet to the men who fought, those rocks meant much more than life or death. Duty was there; honour was there; and in the end victory. And if the smoky curtain that hangs about the field were lifted and the view enlarged, it might be seen that great causes of truth, or justice, or freedom, and long tranquil years in smiling lands depended indeed upon this ragged ridge, made famous by the blundering collision of two armies, worthless except for the tactical purpose of the moment and probably ill-adapted and wrongly selected even for that.[4]

Wage disputes once stood in something like the same oblique relationship to the unspoken, or imperfectly formulated and imperfectly articulated discontent of the working classes, as the lie of the land on a battlefield does to the policies of statesmen and the destinies of nations. Wage disputes fought by organized

[4] W. S. Churchill, *Lord Randolph Churchill*, Macmillan, 1907, p. 466.

labour at one time appeared to be the only form that working-class grievance could take. Issues that seemed to turn on the complex multiplicities and pettifogging niceties of rates of pay, in fact drew their strength and bitterness from ingrained suspicions of the employer and long memories of social, legal, and political subjugation. Wages have always mattered of course; and in the absence of suspicions and memories have always been able to rouse feelings and provoke tempers. But the root problem of labour relations was for long the problem of the relations between the classes. And these had been for long corrupted by the incurable disposition of the minorities which exercised overwhelming social and political ascendancy, to take full advantage of the way in which the institutions of society had been ranged against the community at large so as to place it at a hopeless disadvantage socially, legally, and politically, as well as economically.

The trades union movement was no sooner established than it set about tackling the wider social issues by the strategy of indirect approach. In the end it financed a political party and achieved substantial results for which it nevers gets all the credit that is its due. But it also redoubled its efforts to wrest lasting concessions from employers by direct assault. The efforts were spectacular, achieved results which were in no way commensurate with the disruption they caused, and are inordinately lauded by writers who would no more dream of imputing to union policy costs which were disproportionate to the results achieved than their colleagues would dream of denouncing immensely successful captains of industry because the social and economic consequences of their achievements may have left the world, on balance, worse off than it might have been without them.

It is hard to blame the trades union movement for pursuing a policy of frontal assault which was, in fact, as ineffectual in civil affairs as Liddell Hart later taught the generals to recognize that it was senseless in war. Without being able to claim that it could bring relief which was more immediate and concrete than that promised by Chartism, the movement would doubtless have disintegrated as quickly as Chartism did. Moreover it had to deal with employers who were only really successful at managing their men when hard times had made the men docile. The employer had the same management problem as the general, the cabinet minister, the bishop, or indeed any other leader of men, who could, if he cared to do so, immerse himself in the technicalities of his craft and convince himself that he was doing his job efficiently when he had mastered them. Without some grasp of the appropriate technicalities of his craft no man can reasonably hope to succeed. An aptitude for them—a tactical skill, a mechanical flair, marketing intuition, a head for figures, a talent for casuistry, diplomatic gifts, and the like, can often take a man to the top. But the technicalities of a job, when the job is chiefly a matter of managing men, can easily be the least part of it : the easiest to acquire, the simplest to impart. And in business, as in war, or politics, or religion, the art of management is essentially the art of uniting men in a common purpose. Consequently the businessman who devoted to finance, technology, or marketing, the enthusiasm and expertise that ought to have been devoted to the most intractable of all his problems, the problem of managing men who had ceased to be utterly dependent upon him for work, could not reasonably complain when they revolted at being treated as mere factory-fodder, and made their belligerent dispositions of defence against him.

Frontal assault by means of the wage dispute may be an understandable weakness as well as an irremediable defect of trade union strategy. But it is excessively costly. It denies work to men for whom there can be no employment at the higher rates of pay negotiated by the unions. It compels men with the skill and experience to do the better-paid jobs which they can no longer get or keep, to seek less remunerative work in jobs which demand less than they can give. The waste caused by idleness is thereby compounded by the waste caused by the misuse of skills. And the inevitable over-crowding at each lower level forces other men down another rung of the ladder of employment. Barriers to entry, including the demarcation of boundaries between jobs, reduce opportunities at every level, increase the overcrowding at the bottom, and operate most damagingly against barely tolerated minority groups, and women. Conventions as to the pace of work, as well as agreements about it, which are often as much a part of the wage-bargain as the rate of pay and the definition of the job, further diminish the access of men to work; and withdrawal of labour upon pretexts which range from the common cold at one extreme, to breach of contract by the employer at the other, can frequently put work beyond the reach of all.

Restrictions upon the access of labour to employment, imposed by trades unions in the interests of those who are firmly entrenched in their jobs, are no less detrimental to output than corresponding restrictions upon the access of capital and enterprise to lucrative openings, imposed by established business and professional interests for similar reasons. By an amiable division of labour the task of denouncing the monopolistic practices of business is performed by historians of working-class movements; and the task of admonishing the restrictive practices of trades unions is left to the historians of business: both tasks being performed, apparently, without the least consciousness of the absurdity of rebuking the other side for conduct which is excusable, if not thoroughly admirable, on one's own side, whichever that happens to be.

The chief casualties of all these compacts and arrangements are the unorganized working man, who was in the majority of all working men until recently, and the hapless consumer, who is everyone with money to spend. They have neither historian nor apologist to speak for them and make known the extent to which they have been distrained upon by those who were able to manipulate the terms upon which economic progress was permitted to improve their lives. Locked in combat, or conspiring together to share the spoils, organized capital and organized labour have divided the allegiances of historians and all but completely exhausted their interests.

The ordinary consumer may rate a perfunctory tribute from the historians: he is, after all, the person whose needs are what the entire system of finance and trade, industry and farming, supposedly exists to serve. But like the ordinary constituency voter, the ordinary consumer is more often the victim of those who ostensibly contend for his suffrage, than the arbiter of their fortunes. He is an amateur opposed by professionals; without the knowledge, resources, or organization, to resist their momentum. They bring overwhelming forces to bear against him. When they effect a reconciliation of purposes between themselves; or make collusive arrangements to the immense satisfaction of all concerned, as to the terms upon which men who must work together can do so amicably, despite their mutually antagonistic aims; then such reconciliations and agreements can be depended on to be at the expense of those who are offered the formalities of deference, as the ordinary consumer and the ordinary constituency voter are, without its substance. And historians who applaud their methods or endorse their achievements are doing a service neither to the integrity of their profession nor to the cause of freedom; and without freedom a sane and liberal social system is impossible to sustain.

9   The open society

A sane and liberal social system is not an easy thing to sustain, however, either in theory or in practice.

In theory, social values and political beliefs are not amenable to argument or demonstration. They provide the foundations upon which structures of logic are reared. But the social values and political beliefs upon which the doctrines of liberal democracy repose their authority are surely amongst the most gratuitously perplexing and transparently implausible of any which have ever won the hearts and inspired the hopes of men. And there are few enough to plead for the visionary idealism that animates them. For everyone knows that man is a flawed giant : a creature who stumbles absurdly and cracks his skull just as he is about to cross the threshold to paradise. Remedies for his defects of character are as various as they are disagreeable, and range from doctrines which preach the extirpation of wants as the sovereign cure for disappointment, frustration, grief, and pain, to panaceas which would turn man into an ant in an ants' nest in the interests of social tranquillity. But from the most ancient to the most modern; from the most sophisticated of the precepts of the mortifiers of flesh and spirit, to the most naïve of the auguries of the prophets of technology; these remedies all inculcate the gloomy conviction that there is nothing to be done with man as he is, and that if he is to be delivered from the bondage of his imperfections, then he must be emasculated, dispossessed, denied, and even crushed. The Golden Age may lie in the remote past, or it may be to come. But wherever it is, it is invariably peopled by purged, depersonalized, curiously vacant creatures, who are more like sleepwalkers than fully sentient men; creatures who have been redeemed by the sacrifice of the multitudinous diversity of the human spirit, its insatiable adventurousness, its inexplicable whimsicality, its scepticism and recalcitrance, its creative fecundity, and its vagrant, questing, disrespectful exuberance.

In the light of these cheerless diagnoses and prognostications what could be more astonishing than the emergence, the indomitable survival, and indeed the impenitent vitality of the bizarre notion that every man is, by right, master of his own fate, and of its political corollary that the state is a necessary evil rather than the fulfilment of human destiny on earth? Even in its native English soil the doctrine that the political system is, at bottom, a kind of joint-stock company with limited liability rather than a transcendental force, has been 'more honoured in the breach than the observance'. Elsewhere it has been widely ridiculed and disparaged as the lamentable consequence of a national incapacity for metaphysical speculation.

Nevertheless this vision of political society as a coalition of free men and women voluntarily acting together for purposes of mutual comfort and mutual aid, has inexplicably survived the systematic assaults of those who have devoted immense powers of intellect to the task of vindicating the view, of which Plato was the most formidable exponent, that the social system is a fusion of elements and the state an organism whose service is perfect freedom.

Nor is this all. By some quixotic freak of history the notion that, for political purposes, all who live together in society should be treated as equals once they cease to be children, freely electing their rulers from amongst their number, and freely removing them from office by electing others in their place, after a term of years, has struck root in a world of giant industrial and commercial corporations where political power has been gathered into aggregations of unsurpassed size, unparalleled cohesion, and unimaginably devastating military potential.

There is no necessary connection between the belief that the power of the state ought to be limited by the rights of the citizen, and the belief that all citizens should enjoy equal political rights. The democratic notion that for essential political purposes the common humanity that men share matters infinitely more than differences of temperament and character, and disparities of endowment and skill, undoubtedly commits those who hold it to strong views about such things as universal suffrage and the secret ballot. But it does not in the least commit them to the view that the political obligations of citizenship are limited, in the last resort, by discretionary rights which individual citizens are free to exercise in defiance of the authority of the state. The state that grants equality of political status to all its citizens may not do so because it takes a libertarian view of its origins and purposes. On the contrary it may very well take a strictly authoritarian view of such matters as it does in countries under communism. In this respect it may simply be following Rousseau who proclaimed the equality of man but subordinated everyone to the General Will, rather than Locke who distinguished between men but gave them all a generous latitude in deciding, at the last, when the state was causing them more trouble than they thought it worth.

In the liberal countries of the world, however, the prevailing belief upon which all political controversy depends for its common ground, combines the conviction that the individual, not the state, is the fundamental unit of politics, with the further conviction that government may be necessary, and even positively desirable, without acquiring any sanction for its activities which is more exalted than that exercised by a public utility.

In practice, there is no state, however liberal its professions, where political authority is held in check by the scruples and restraints implicit in these beliefs. What chance, indeed, has so chastening a creed against the formidable majesty of the state, which can so readily mobilize the passionate tribal and conformist instincts of mankind, purge and elevate them, and then concentrate and direct them to its purposes by exposing them to the glamorous melodrama of its institutional ritual and pageantry, the solemn splendour of its traditions, the funded wisdom of its processes, and the awful menace of its displeasure?

Moreover states differ from one another far less than they appear to do. Common problems afflict them whatever their declared political allegiances; and common problems when they occur in communities which are roughly comparable in social, economic, and political development, drive governments which subscribe to very different political creeds, to make very similar provision for their treatment. Political philosophers profess to be able to see fundamental differences between states, which they trace to an irreconcilable contrariety in the foundations of political obligation. But what are their fastidious distinctions of theory worth compared with the fact that the incessant practical con-

cerns of politics, in countries which differ radically in matters
of political theory, are nevertheless very similar in all of them,
are tackled in very similar ways, and therefore throw up practitioners of the art of handling the people that matter, so as to
achieve intended political results with least friction, whose skills,
suitably modified, could probably be exercised as successfully
abroad as at home?

Social and political pressures pose similar problems in all such
countries; the dispositions prescribed by the military make similar
demands and create similar political interests; and similarities in
the structure of farming, industry, and commerce, limit the range
of political manoeuvre in similar ways. The bureaucrats in such
countries are no less affected by problems, and methods of tackling
them, which transcend political frontiers than the politicians.
And when they meet professional counterparts from countries
as technologically advanced and politically mature as their own,
they are no less acutely conscious than the politicians, of shared experiences which bind them into an international freemasonry,
as well as of loyalties which force them into rivalry and may very
well turn them into enemies.

In this respect the closest affinities of politics are with business,
where rivalry compels firms to adopt methods of production and
forms of organization which differ so little from one firm to the
next that men who leave their own firm for its near rival in order
to better themselves, find no difficulty whatsoever in settling to
routines, methods, and systems, whose details are all that is new to
them.

In every age of history, indeed, the social, political, and economic organization of rival groups has tended towards a common
pattern. Documenting this pattern is one of the commonplace
functions of historical writing. And no one would dispute the
existence of such patterns in any age but his own. The present,
however, is never exempt from the historical process. And democratic countries which pay homage to Locke rather than to
Rousseau have more in common with systems of government
which they vehemently repudiate than their passionate expressions
of abhorrence might lead anyone to suspect who was not acutely
wary of the rhetoric of public objurgation.

This is the fundamental dilemma of modern liberal democratic
politics. It is the dilemma that inevitably arises when political

aspiration is at war with the realities of politics instead of being a reclaimed or expurgated version of them. Accordingly communities which are dedicated to the belief that everyone who is not a criminal, a lunatic, or a child, should be free to take part in politics; that in politics, in Coleridge's phrase, people should be counted and not weighed; and that individuals, in the last analysis, matter more than governments, because it is for their sakes alone that government exists; are inevitably threatened by dangers, afflicted by weaknesses, and assailed by temptations, which can thwart their efforts to achieve their exalted ambitions more easily than they can thwart the efforts of communities whose political ambitions are more prosaic.

Everything conspires against liberal democracy. Instinct is against it. Property is against it. The call of tradition is against it. The claims of race and creed are against it. The interests of class are against it. The urgent needs of commerce and industry are against it. Above all the ambitions of all who covet power are against it.

Liberal democracy is indeed all too easily dominated by those who have the wealth, personality, or connections, with which to decide what are to be the public issues of politics; to manipulate the machinery of representation; and to mould opinion by dint of their mastery of means of indoctrination unequalled in potency since the days when an universal church controlled education, determined questions of religion, morals, and politics, sat in judgment upon the most private concerns of individuals, instructed the cosmopolitan classes in an international language, spoke to the common man in his native tongue, and used its swarms of local agents to justify a dispensation which maintained this extraordinary structure in its commanding position.

Liberal democracy is intensely susceptible to doctrines and blandishments which render majority opinion sacrosanct. Where majority opinion is treated in this way, the state is set decisively above the individual because it becomes the vehicle of an unimpeachable popular will. And minorities which presume to cling to convictions which have failed to gain the suffrage of the majority, stand rebuked by implication, courting serious trouble at times when social pressure can make common cause with what are alleged to be the needs of the safety of the state.

Modern technology has liberal democracy at its mercy. Military and business interests, never at a loss for argument in support of claims for preferential treatment, can easily delude a public trained, if at all, to suspect only the specious advocacy of an earlier and simpler age, into believing that modern war and modern business make such demands upon resources as to justify unprecedented scope and protection for their activities. In fact the appeal to technology adds nothing but modern instances to the hoary sophistries about defence, prestige, and economic and political expediency, that reconciled earlier generations to the devouring appetites of these interests.

Military protection, like police protection, can never be absolute. But safety, like security, is something that communities can generally have in greater measure than before, simply by devoting more intelligence and more resources to it than they had done hitherto. In the end the quest for safety will turn society into a cross between a fortress and a concentration camp. Many political communities would not be much altered by the change. But liberal democracy cannot pay this price for safety without sacrificing everything that makes safety worthwhile. Freedom makes many demands upon those who value it: accepting a measure of vulnerability is one of them.

The claims of business are subtler and more insidious. Business has only emerged as a sustained political force in public life since the Industrial Revolution. Before the Industrial Revolution, when land was virtually the sole criterion of wealth and standing, the political system chiefly benefited those with a good deal of it. The advent of business as the dominant influence in politics has naturally changed the issues of politics. But it has not changed the objectives of politics.

Businessmen are as anxious as the landlords were before them to turn society into a paradise for all who own or control the larger aggregations of the dominant form of property, and sell the greater volume of the dominant types of goods and services. And they handle the familiar arguments with equal skill. Like the landlords they are great patriots, and claim the right to reward themselves handsomely at the public expense for putting weapons into the hands of the military, just as their predecessors had claimed the right to reward themselves with Corn Laws for cultivating the arable so as to raise stalwarts for the infantry. Like the landlords they are preoccupied with the need to preserve the social order that enables them to thrive, and therefore support policies, as their predecessors did, which provide enough work to keep the population employed, without at the same time destroying the efficacy of the threat of the sack. When they cannot appeal to the needs of defence, or public welfare, in support of their claims for preferential treatment, their patriotism once more comes to their rescue and they appeal instead to national prestige, which would be irretrievably dishonoured, in their opinion, should the country come to depend upon foreign suppliers of whatever it is that they happen to do or make.

This appeal may seem to draw its strength from the curious assumption that the fair name of a civilized community depends, in some crucial way, upon the number and variety of the things it does or makes rather than upon the quality of the life its citizens lead. But it is shrewdly calculated to catch even the least fearful and most melifluously plausible of politicians at a point of acute sensitivity. For it is a reminder that constituency favours are never inalienable. Any industry which petitions for special treatment, in effect makes the humiliating confession that it cannot stand competition. And any industry which petitions, provided that it is a big enough employer of labour, must be heeded, if only because those who work in it will use their votes with a will against any government which throws them to the wolves. In economically advanced countries, where capital is supplanting labour, this means that declining industries in which the work force is, by definition, comparatively large, will exert a political influence out of all proportion to the number of their employees and the value of their contribution to the national product.

But there are always unanswerable reasons for making an exception for every big industry which applies for help, and for excusing the manoeuvres of every business which uses its economic strength or its political influence to keep rivals out of its markets.

That competition is an excellent thing is the unvarying theme of all who speak for business on public occasions. When they enlarge upon this theme they do so by praising the facility with which competition can ensure that businesses use resources with an economy which reflects their relative scarcity; by paying tribute to the specialization of function that grows out of the application of competitive business skills to problems of scarcity;

and by extolling international trade for carrying competition round the world, forcing the remotest businesses to make the most of local resources in the light of what is being done elsewhere, creating specialisms, diversifying economies, and thus enabling the ordinary consumer to lay the entire world under contribution in his search for the cheapest markets in which to supply his needs.

Competition, however, though an excellent thing, is always for others. Arrangements between companies which restrict competition are hailed by their authors as triumphs of enterprise. Practices which foster consumer loyalty at the expense of competition are defended by their beneficiaries in the name of liberty. And foreign competition is always unfair competition, particularly when it happens to succeed. When Lancashire clothed the world it was a magnificent vindication of English skill and business acumen which an invigorating and wholesome competitive system had rewarded with higher wages than foreign competitors could pay and higher profits than they could earn. When Japan eclipsed Lancashire it was a sinister portent of what could be done with cheap labour. A country which had organized its teeming millions to do one thing better than its competitors must presently be able to do everything better. The apostles of competition, stampeded by the logic of their macabre hallucinations, soon despaired of the beneficient workings of the system they had so recently acclaimed. No longer did they declare that everyone must benefit in the end when things are made and sold more cheaply than ever before. No longer did they scout the idea that any one country could reduce its competitors to industrial nonentity by being able to do everything better than they could. Demoralization, it seems, had banished from their minds all recollection of the arguments that were once so telling. They forgot that even the most efficient economy must buy its competitors' goods and services, or at any rate the goods and services of those to whom its competitors sell, unless it prefers giving its products away to selling them. And they forgot that, in fact, efficient economies have no choice, if they wish to remain efficient, but to concentrate their resources upon the things they do preeminently well, and leave their competitors to do the things that they could perhaps do as well, if not even better, but only at the cost of sacrificing some part of their output of the things in which their pre-eminence is unchallengeable.

Efficiency, however, is only a means to an end. It is the paramount factor in business planning only when competition is so effectual that firms cannot survive without it. And there will always be easier ways of making a living whilst businessmen and politicians can play upon universal fears by expressing ominous and preferably unspecified forebodings about the future, and by conjuring the harrowing apparitions of bankruptcy and unemployment out of the past, to such effect that everyone is reduced to a state of mind in which he is ready to perceive a necessary connexion between prosperity and protection.

Protection means putting up with second-best. If it did not, there would be no need for protection. The consumer must pay more, and probably pay more for worse. Protection also means depriving industry of the discipline of competition. In its protected environment, industry luxuriates; and giant firms presently emerge to dominate domestic markets and rejoice the hearts of all true patriots. These firms are always got up to look magnificent; but their magnificence always, apparently, requires the support of protection; for protection, once conceded, is never subsequently given up. And the consumer is therefore once more the loser.

In rich countries his losses are a small matter if there is compensating gain in other directions. But protection often defeats its own declared ends. When the landlords engineered high prices for corn the infantry got starvelings not stalwarts. When Germany subsidized its steel exports Britain got its merchant navy on the cheap. And once its barriers become formidable, protection itself becomes competitive, with every sovereign state threatening rivals with its commercial thunderbolts, and hawking its commercial bargains from one diplomatic conference to the next, to the growing consternation of all who had looked to protection for the stabilization of the market.

The chief objection, however, to any policy which strengthens one section of the community at the expense of the rest, has nothing to do with its pernicious effect upon the section strengthened, or even with its repercussions upon the living standards of the rest of the community. Any policy which confers exceptional power, in its appointed sphere, upon an active and determined section of the community, in fact confers upon it privileged

L

access to political power. To some extent, indeed, policy merely ratifies a *fait accompli*; for privileged access is usually achieved by those who have already succeeded in exercising some part of the undue influence they are bent on institutionalizing. When land was the chief source of wealth and political power the landlords did not dominate society because they controlled parliament; they controlled parliament because they dominated society. Industry has never exercised a social influence comparable with that once exercised by land; but throughout the world prodigious aggregations of industrial power tower over the political life of the communities they exist to serve, in democratic and totalitarian states alike. Their fortunes are a vital question of politics; their needs and wishes are earnestly consulted and sedulously attended to; protection shields them from rough-handling. Whether they are publicly accountable or not is scarcely more than a trifling matter of bureaucratic convenience : for public money invariably keeps them going when they falter, and central planning decides their future development whatever the formalities of their status.

In many quarters, central planning, the comprehensive authority wielded by a handful of politicians and businessmen over the disposition of the resources of some huge industry or some vast region, is rapturously acclaimed as the secret of the rejuvenation of capitalism since the war. Those who invest central planning with providential qualities, blandly ignore the inherent, incorrigible, and fatal defects of central planning, to which an immense literature of economic analysis and much historical experience bear witness. And they ignore something of infinitely greater importance. They ignore the fact that the social system is indivisible : that economic liberalism is the reciprocal of political liberalism; and that without the rigorous discipline of competition business will quickly get out of hand, to the lasting detriment of the freedom of the individual.

Those who urge the case for central planning and extol the virtues of monopolistic competition utterly fail to see that liberal communities can no more tolerate the rank growth of interests powerful enough to be able to bring massive influence to bear upon government, and to compromise the freedom of choice, and independence, of the individual consumer, wage-earner, businessman, or professional worker, than it can tolerate violence, graft, and jobbery, in public life. They fail to see that economic efficiency is not enough, even were theirs an infallible prescription for it. And they fail to see that if central planning has rejuvenated anything, since the war, it is not capitalism, in the sense of a system based upon competitive free enterprise, which it has rejuvenated, but a coalition of interests resolutely devoted to the purpose of creating conditions in which competition can be progressively enfeebled and finally suppressed. To the extent that it succeeds it must provoke aggressive reaction from disconcerted interests organized and articulate enough to make their resistance felt; and in the internecine warfare that ensues the commonwealth dissolves into an anarchy of vociferously contentious and recalcitrant antagonisms.

In practice the commonwealth does not dissolve. Antagonisms are more or less reconciled. But interests triumph over the public interest; and hopes for the future of liberal democracy are destroyed. Those who welcome this revival of baronial warfare, with its formal manoeuvres and ritual truces brought up to date, or at any rate refuse to denounce it, contend that it reflects the realities of modern commercial and industrial life and that it is the duty of politics to accommodate the issues of public debate to these realities.

No doubt politics have always done the bidding of interests powerful enough to make their own special needs and wishes the leading public issues of the day. But what hope can there be for liberal democracy if the future, in this essential respect, is destined to be no better than the past? And what salvation can there be for the individual in a political system which recognizes only the embattled might of organized interests and responds only to the pressure that they can exert?

In the nineteenth century the realities of commercial and industrial life swept the politicians of Europe first one way and then the other, without ever inspiring them to do very much about the realities that dominated the lives of those who were not lucky enough to be able to profit by the concessions that business demanded and obtained. When industry raised the cry of *laissez-faire*, *laissez-faire* was, in fact, the slogan of the fox in the henhouse. But politicians bowed to the realities and conformed to the proclaimed needs of business without concerning themselves unduly as to the needs of those who bought the adulterated products

L*

of industry, endured the contaminating effects of industry, sold their labour in circumstances of overwhelming disadvantage, or got themselves killed, injured, made idle, or otherwise overtaken by misfortune, as a result of industrialization. *Laissez-faire* was no charter of liberties for them. When times changed, business, ably abetted by the military, demanded protection and got it. All over Europe politicians found excellent reasons for doing their bidding. In the end they did so even in Britain. But protection was the signal for a campaign of systematic exploitation of everyone who was not lucky enough to be on the side of the predators. In the twisted language of politics, protection was the euphemism for oppression. And with the passing of this simulacrum of economic liberalism, the chances of political liberalism were fatally compromised. Another age of benevolent despotism dawned; for organized labour had to be propitiated, and the price exacted by organized labour for its complicity in the unholy alliance of business with the state was welfare.

Welfare has never meant lavish and compassionate support for those in greatest need. Nor did it mean, until recently, an indiscriminate and unmeasured largesse : a surcharged cornucopia from which the strong and intrepid can take much, and the weak, hesitant, timorous, or inadequate, may, if they are unlucky, get little or nothing. But whatever it meant in terms of tangible relief, the ultimate effect of welfare was to get governments everywhere deeply involved in affairs whose administration committed them beyond their power to withstand subsequent pressure to intervene further and more widely. Accordingly, governments which began by protecting industries, presently found themselves supporting them, and even running them, when they were not, in effect, being run by them. Governments which intervened in the economic process in order to house the homeless and find work for the workless, presently found themselves controlling rents, and then building the homes that the commercial builders no longer had the incentive to supply, settling wage-claims by appeal to those scholastic abstractions of theory whose labyrinthine ingenuities are now the commonplaces of arbitrated wage-negotiation, and even attempting to raise the general level of business activity, when it sank lower than they thought it should by doing contradictory things, and getting the volume, timing, and even direction, of their efforts so horribly wrong that in the end any success they may have had was entirely due to the urge, or the need, to prepare the country for war.

Benevolent despotism now prevails everywhere and permeates political thinking everywhere. Anyone who seriously questions its efficacy or its political morality runs the risk of forfeiting his influence in politics. Yet its articles of faith offend against crucial principles of liberal democracy. Benevolent despotism shelters and supports industrial and commercial enterprises, and connives at the restrictive practices of professional bodies and organized labour, instead of exposing them all to competition, making them liable for all the costs their operations incur, and enforcing competition whenever it shows signs of weakening. It pampers and chaperons the individual by doing many things for him which, as a free citizen, he should be expected to do for himself. It humbugs him into believing that the resources with which these things are done have been either conjured out of the air by a transcendentally inspired government, or expropriated from the rich by a magnanimously solicitous one. In fact the mass of ordinary citizens might, with justice, echo the complaint voiced by a vituperative pamphleteer of the later Middle Ages who denounced the Venetians and Florentines for buying English wool on credit, selling it for cash, and making such good use of the proceeds that they 'wipe our nose with our own sleeve'. And by giving help in kind rather than in money benevolent despotism administers the culminating insult of taking it for granted that the ordinary citizen is too reckless, ineffectual, or foolish, to be given any choice as to how he should order his life. In the perennial controversy waged by those who contend that society must be protected from classes which lack the training and experience to act responsibly, with those who urge that exercising responsibility is the only known way of developing a sense of responsibility, benevolent despotism endorses the arguments with which countless generations of the propertied classes have resisted the importunities of the masses, and takes sides against the values upon which liberal democracy depends.

Any régime of thought and policy, once it establishes its intellectual and emotional ascendancy over public life, tends to be self-perpetuating. Everything conspires to favour it. Every success fortifies it; and even failure, unless it is outrageously discreditable, ignominious, or clumsy, can always be turned to its advantage by those who are astute enough to perceive the cause of failure in a want of vigour and perseverance in the application of the régime's favourite remedies. These remedies are then applied with a will; and so complex is the interaction of things that, in the congenial climate of opinion that sustains it, an established régime can generally dissemble the harm done by its favourite remedies, and parade their beneficial consequences to such effect that opposition is baffled and silenced, if not actually won over, and popularity in other quarters is assured. Its remedies may be applied with a will; but they will only rarely be applied with much consistency; and only at the peril of the future of the régime will they be applied against those upon whom the régime depends. Since life is a complex riddle to which there are no simple clues, it is, perhaps, as well that no system gets a clear run unless it resorts to violence. And when it does resort to violence, in order to rid itself of critics and opponents with enough political power to embarrass it seriously, its use of violence gets immediate results, as a rule, at the cost of jeopardizing the conditions in which those results can be fruitful. In the end, therefore, every régime which is not actually overthrown by force, is discredited by the atrocities, the scandals, the prevarications, and the inconsistencies, that prepare the way for the successor which can exploit its failures, its inadequacies, and its loss of nerve.

When the strong oppress the weak because the state has failed to provide an environment in which competition can work, the obvious remedy is to correct the faults in the environment that make it impossible for competition to work. But this solution made very little appeal to the beneficiaries of *laissez-faire* when *laissez-faire* was the prevailing doctrine of politics. And now that *laissez-faire* is a thing of the past it makes even less of an appeal to those who invariably want to cancel the harm done when competition is suppressed by imposing some form of public accountability upon business and trades unions in the name of liberal democracy. Public accountability, however, is not the reasonable and liberal solution it appears to be. It centralizes power which should be dispersed. It gives the state authority over matters better left to the market because, lacking omniscience, the state cannot hope to rival the multiplicity of informed individual judgments which the market can reflect. And it installs at the heart of the political system organizations which have already shown how astutely they are capable of exploiting the deficiencies of the political system, and gives them incomparable opportunities of bringing undue pressure to bear at points of acutely sensitive political susceptibility.

Those who denounce competition rightly claim that monopoly is the inevitable result of leaving everyone to his own devices. But competition is not simply a matter of leaving everyone to his own devices. Competition is not simply another name for the abdication by government of its active role in economic affairs. On the contrary competition soon lapses when government fails to enforce it; and when the failure of competition is used as a pretext for government intervention in the economic process, political freedom is the next casualty. Where the system needs discipline, it gets control; where economic power needs to be dispersed, its concentration is reinforced. And when government has failed the community by conferring its patronage upon monopolistic businesses and professions instead of doing its best to cancel the privileges they have contrived for themselves, what can the trades unions do but take up the weapons which have served business and the professions so well and use them as best they may? The thunderous threats that issue from one side are matched by the commination uttered by the other; violence is met by violence; and the ordinary citizen stands by, even as he did in the reign of Stephen, fearful for his family and for his future, whilst the lances break and the swords flash, and the land is given over to anarchy until the next truce is declared and the contestants, one of whom is often enough his lawfully elected government, depart to recover from the last encounter and prepare themselves for the next.

But if political freedom is threatened by the pressure of monopolistic businesses, professions, and organizations of wage-earners, acting either independently or in concert with the state; if it is threatened by the insidiously seductive attractions of welfare dispensed by public authorities in the name of justice and humanity; it is also threatened, in a sense, by those who would be its friends. Those who oppose widespread public intervention in the lives of ordinary citizens, however disinterested its motive, almost invariably weaken the case against intervention by stressing the incorrigible incompetence of public authorities in economic affairs, their unflattering record as forecasters of com-

munity needs, and the ponderous, blundering, and obtuse ways
in which they have always gone about their task of trying to meet
the needs and satisfy the wishes of those whom they have entered
the market to serve. No doubt what they say is perfectly true. But
critics who stress the practical limitations of public action draw
attention away from the most serious of the counts against it.

Compared with its effects upon political freedom the effects of
public intervention upon economic efficiency scarcely matter at
all. It matters far more, if it is true, to know that public intervention, carried beyond a certain point, will stultify the initiative
and drain the self-reliant vigour of those who should provide the
community with its Hampdens, its Wilkes, its Cobbetts, and its
Cobdens. In a political system whose vitality depends upon the
alert and intelligent participation of everyone who is entitled to
vote, it matters tremendously that the ordinary citizen should
develop and exercise an educated and independent judgment in
political affairs; a thing that he can scarcely be expected to do
if in the most intimate concerns of his private life his power of
decision is taken from him by those who, in the insolence of power,
take it for granted that they know better than he does himself
what is best for him, and who make themselves responsible,
through the educational system, for providing him with the
attitudes, and with much of the vocational training, that he will
carry with him for the rest of his life. And above all it matters
for the future of political freedom that no government should ever
be allowed to acquire such power over the lives of those whom it
represents and professes to serve, as to be able to restore, for the
most enlightened and generous-hearted reasons imaginable, the
inquisitorial surveillance that the Catholic Church once imposed
in its efforts to promote the sentiments expressed in the Sermon
on the Mount, and recent totalitarian political régimes have
imposed in the name of the Brotherhood of Man.

Those who are too poor, or ill, or oppressed, to be able to think
clearly for themselves, no doubt require, and should get, all the
help that public authorities can give. At a period when pressure
upon space threatens the beauty of the countryside and the
amenity of life in towns, no doubt public authorities must submit
all sorts of activities to control which in other circumstances they
should not attempt to regulate or constrict. And in a world of
monopolies where the consumer is relieved of his freedom of

choice in what are purported to be the interests of rationalization, scale economies, professional standards of conduct, and the like, the public authorities no doubt have some excuse for trying to do for large sections of the community what few are capable of doing for themselves. But in a political system in which competition works, and in which commercial undertakings pay the full social costs of their activities, because the public authorities have done their duty by making them compete and pay, then it is for the ordinary citizen and not for the public authorities to decide whether he is to have present goods or future goods, whether he is to have a home or a holiday, whether he is to buy insurance or a cottage by the sea, whether he is to work or to idle, whether he is to be cured of some troublesome and possibly fatal disease, or to eat, drink, and be merry, and then cease upon the midnight with a certain amount of pain.

Restoring competition to economic activities, and freedom of choice to the individual citizen, are essential to the political health of any community which subscribes to the values from which liberal democracy derives its strength. Without competition and choice liberty will be progressively circumscribed through the joint workings of monopoly and welfare; and the ordinary citizen, as he grows richer, will presently find that he has been turned into a slave. Ironically enough his slavery will have been dearly bought because wealth presumably grows more slowly in an environment which offers institutionalized resistance to economic change than it does when competition sets the pace. Richer, however, he will undoubtedly be. And his affluence will liberate him from a thousand brutalizing cares. But it will not necessarily stir in him a passion for political liberty. A man must needs have a full stomach and a warm bed before he can think about politics or care about liberty. Only the rarest spirits are not utterly cast down for want of such things. In that sense economic development is an indispensable prerequisite for political emancipation. But it takes an unusually ingenuous and complacent materialism to assume that where affluence is, there liberal democracy will quicken, or thrive.

Affluence as pervasive as it is in the richest countries today is without precedent in history. In such countries industrialization has lifted even the poorest and least favoured classes above the hopeless misery and unutterable destitution of other times and other places. But affluence itself is not new. Social classes have been affluent before now. And if we want to know how affluence will affect the classes that are rich for the first time, how can we do better than inquire as to how it affected those who were rich, or at any rate comfortable, in the past? History is full of their doings: the record is plain for all to see. Can we be reassured by what it reveals? Is there cause for complacency, or optimism, or even for moderate hope? Does not the conduct, public and private, of those who enjoyed all the leisure that there was to be had, who were educated in the most favourable circumstances, and given the finest opportunities to cultivate mind and spirit, surely lead the dispassionate observer to confirm Acton's dictum that every class is unfit to govern? Does it not bode ill for the prospects of liberal democracy once monopoly and welfare have acquired a stranglehold over the community?

Liberal democracy is not simply a matter of expressing the popular will through the medium of representative institutions by enabling the elecorate to vote into power the politicians who offer the most promising likelihood of carrying that will into effect. No government, not even the most unrepresentative, deliberately sets out to flout the popular will. Most, whatever their political complexion, work exceedingly hard to gratify or at least to conciliate it, if not to persuade it that what they have done, or intend to do, in fact fulfils its wishes or serves its best interests. In this respect one form of government is very like another. Government is not even necessarily democratic simply because it submits the boundless ambitions and extravagant policies of those who crave for political power to the humbling penitential disciplines of the representative system. Regulating political antagonisms so that governments can be changed in accordance with a constitutionally established routine of succession, instead of having to be overthrown by violence when they are no longer tolerable, undoubtedly makes for social tranquillity. But it readily degenerates into systematic collusion between political adversaries to exclude vital issues from public debate. And this enables politicians to turn public controversy into a solemn farce in much the same way as the self-imposed restraints upon competition between industrial giants turns rivalry in the shops into another kind of solemn farce, the solemn farce of product differentiation.

Representative institutions are not even more effectual as a curb to the temptation to exercise an unlimited despotism in politics than the curb to which all politicians already answer whatever the political system over which they preside. Those who rule are seldom unconstrained in what they do, whatever the power they appear to possess. They are always few, and always dependent upon the support of others who are politically influential because of their faculty for manipulating the machinery of politics, and who will withdraw their support the moment things are done, or proposed, which disappoint their expectations, or jeopardize their own positions by alienating important groups below them. Sometimes those who rule can reach out, over the heads of the factions and the coalitions, as generations of laurelled conquerors and demagogues have been able to do, and address their ringing appeals directly to the ravening appetites of the masses. But the characteristic posture of the ordinary average ruler is less reminiscent of the swagger of the grandiloquent hero than it is of the glazed immobility of the ass of Buridan, paralysed between two equal bales of hay; for whatever the régime, and whatever the needs of the hour, government policy is almost invariably a makeshift compromise between an irreducible element of popular will, bureaucratic momentum, and the vagaries of the active groups upon which government depends.

And when government action most obviously expresses the popular will its action may very well be a triumphant vindication of democracy without being in the least liberal. Indeed the more popular the government, the more nearly indisputable its authority; and the greater its authority, the more inquisitorial, inflexible, and extortionate, it can be. Any sort of truculence or contumacy it can visit with the fearful sanction of its representative authority. It can pursue races, or classes, or persons, who dispute its measures, or offend against its decrees, with an intensity of relentless ferocity which more autocratic governments could dare to resort to only in an extremity of danger or provocation. Democracy may be the easy way to make the popular will politically enforceable; but it has precious little to do with liberalism. And it is to liberal democracy that the free world has committed itself.

Liberalism is, essentially, respect for the individual expressed politically as absence of government. It means leaving the individual citizen to make his own decisions, to think as he will, to act as he likes. In another age this might be construed as a licence for anarchy. But in an age when the political appeal of social problems has been made irresistible by universal suffrage and the party system that goes with it, the danger is not that governments will do too little but that they will do too much.

There are many things that governments must obviously do for everyone, because no one can possibly do them for himself; and there are many people whom governments must help, and should help generously, because they are obviously beyond the scope or reach of private care and commercial insurance. But it is a fallacious extension of this reasoning to argue that governments ought therefore to do many of the things that people can very well do for themselves, and should do for themselves if they want them done; and to contend, furthermore, that governments have a duty to do them because, given the choice, such things are always better done by public agency than by private initiative.

Liberal democracy, if it is to work as it should, depends upon a very great deal of active control of the affairs of the nation being exercised by governments which are sufficiently independent of even the most formidable interests as to be able to discipline them in the public interest. This means calling upon governments to provide conditions in which politicians will compete publicly and peaceably for the suffrage of ordinary men and women instead of settling everything between themselves behind closed doors, or simply mustering their supporters and fighting it out in the streets. It means creating elective bodies of one sort or another with enough real authority delegated to them to encourage ordinary people to take part in the running of the community instead of allowing themselves to become more and more habituated to the idea that their role in government is confined to the casting of votes. It means taking steps to prevent competition from degenerating into a series of conspiracies in restraint of trade. It means forbidding compulsory associations of all kinds except where the necessity for professional standards makes it essential that all practitioners of a craft should be subject to a measure of supervision. It means unstinted help for the necessitous, and a fiscal policy designed to reduce the distance between the classes so as to diminish the political influence of wealth and status.

But if liberty is to flourish, if it is not merely to survive as a residual category, then the levelling measures dictated by the desire to equalize treatment, or opportunity, must be weighed against the inevitable constraints they impose. The cause of equality is often better served indeed by measures which set people free by releasing the forces of competition when these have been constrained, than by measures which meet constraint with further constraint, restriction with further restriction. But at some point the demands of liberty and equality are bound to diverge and even become incompatible. There is no formal solution in politics to the problem of reconciling their respective claims. Liberty, however, cannot flourish unless governments forbear to do many things that they have the power and even, perhaps, the authority to do. Hence the final test of a liberal democracy is neither the legitimacy of its authority, nor the popularity of its policies. What it refrains from doing matters as much as what it does. Indeed in a sense it matters more, because inaction is so characteristic and incorrigible a feature of government that nothing is easier than to mistake an honourable scruple as to the wisdom or rectitude of intervention for procrastination, duplicity, and neglect; and nothing is more tempting to a politician than the chance to make party capital out of any disinclination to act, whatever its motive.

Moreover whatever governments do to promote equality makes an appeal which is inherently more compelling than anything they can do to promote liberty. Reforms which open prospects of greater equality to an electorate in which inequalities are slight enough to cause concern, have the irresistible quality of making what seems to be an unmistakably tangible contribution to emancipation and enlightenment. Reforms which strengthen or extend the liberty of the subject, however, usually do so by removing obstacles and dismantling obstructions, by annulling agreements, disrupting 'arrangements', harassing conspiratorial networks of kindred spirits bent on mutual aid at the public expense, exposing public issues to public scrutiny, and thereby creating disturbance, causing vexation where there was contentment, and aggravating instability. Reforms such as these cannot fail to be decried by some critics as very mixed blessings, and to be soundly condemned by others who brand any change radical enough to involve the abolition of usages which are hallowed in their sight because they have lasted for a long time, as a clumsy, intemperate, and uncomprehending violation of the sanctity of a social structure which had been served and enriched by untold generations of forbears. The usages may have lasted for a long time simply because they admirably suited the purposes of those in every generation who benefited by the exclusiveness they safe-guarded and promoted. But critics who welcome reform only when it leaves things very much as they were, are not to be deterred from defending those whose background, outlook, and interests conspire to spoil their appetite for change, in such a way as to make it harder to liberate the community than it is to strengthen the bonds that tie it down.

It may be tempting for countries which subscribe to the tenets of liberal democracy to ignore the claims of liberty in their pur-suit of the cause of equality. But it takes some fortitude in the twentieth century to assume that, if they succumb to temptation, there will be no price to pay. All over Europe, in the twentieth century, in war and in peace, when Leviathan stirs there is dark-ness at noon, and the nightmare world of Kafka's novels becomes an everyday reality for those who oppose Leviathan, or perhaps merely displease it unintentionally. If the lights of civilization can go out so quickly in Europe can we be so sure that they will always shine elsewhere? No written constitution, however rigorous, categorical, and explicit its formulation, is more depend-able than the men appointed to interpret or enforce it; and how many men are proof against major aberrations of political opinion, or against those wild gusts of anger and recrimination that sweep through the political life of apparently stable com-munities and leave havoc in their wake? A liberal democracy, with its mass electorate, is not less susceptible to political mad-ness than other systems of government. Many would claim that it is more so. Consequently the final test of its quality must be the quality of the habits of mind and character that ordinary men and women bring to their political responsibilities.

In the end intangible things matter most: a steadfast refusal to believe that the sense of certainty is a sufficient test of the validity of a set of beliefs; respect amounting to passion for the privacy of others; a profound conviction that no man is good enough to be another man's master except for severely limited practical purposes; an unremitting suspicion of everything huge and imposing, and of everyone who appears to be larger than life; distrust of all experts because expertise is an incitement to authoritarianism in politics; deference to all minorities; toleration of muddle and inconsistency in public life because life is not consistent and the nooks and crannies harbour idiosyncracy and creativity as well as the more prosaic laxities; and hatred of cruelty and oppression, whatever the provocation, in all their manifold forms.

If this is an inadequate list, then the fault is its author's; but if it is a negative list that is because liberal democracy is essentially a negative creed. It acts only to free men and women from constraints. It does not presume to know better than they do how they should order their lives. Government, however, is a continuing need, because freedom is always under threat from an unexpected quarter, and universal preoccupation with problems which are fast receding conceals from all but the sharpest eyes the nature and momentousness of the emergent issues that call for immediate attention. Moreover as circumstances change, the triumphs of the past hang like mill-stones round the necks of those who are trying to liberalize society by grappling with fresh difficulties and new menaces. Change, indeed, is one of the few constants in politics. Few welcome change except perhaps in the first flowering of manhood or womanhood. None can predict its course. But all change grows out of the past; and the study of the past has come to be one of the major intellectual disciplines of the age. Its concern with social and political issues invites the hope that it may not be without its lessons, despite Kierkegaard's sardonic apophthegm that we live forwards but understand backwards.

The hope is vain because history, for all the impressive authority of its pronouncements, is not what it seems to be. But those who write history are not so restricted by the limitations of their medium that they have no choice but to lend their authority to a view of social values which inculcates the conviction that totalitarianism is best because it gets things done, that success is its own justification, that the most important rewards in life are the ones that you can touch and see, and that the most important classes are the ones that achieve these rewards. Freedom and toleration are the highest of the political aspirations as love and friendship are the greatest of the private ones. Freedom and toleration are always in danger; and never more so than in periods when society feels the need to close ranks against its enemies. In such periods, panic can quickly destroy the constructive work of years : the climate of opinion is such that people are easily stampeded. Historians have a modest role in creating that climate of opinion. The contention of this book is that they are using it to create a climate of opinion which makes freedom and toleration harder to maintain when they might be doing something to make it easier.

Index